T0194286

TWO HEARTS IN THE WORLD WAR II

UNDERSTANDING THE EVIL AND GOOD

WALTER JURASZEK

WESTBOW
PRESS®
A DIVISION OF THOMAS NELSON
& ZONDERVAN

WestBow Press books may be ordered through booksellers or by contacting:

WestBow Press
A Division of Thomas Nelson & Zondervan
1663 Liberty Drive
Bloomington, IN 47403
www.westbowpress.com
1 (866) 928-1240

ISBN: 978-1-9736-5104-8 (sc)
ISBN: 978-1-9736-5105-5 (e)

Print information available on the last page.

WestBow Press rev. date: 04/16/2019

THE FIFTH COLUMN IN CARPATHIAN MOUNTAIN IN THE SOUTHERN POLAND

The Fifth Column became a known fact in literature, but also in the minds of many European nations. The organization and birth of the Fifth Column was initiated during the Spanish Civil War. General Francisco Franco coined the phrase Fifth Column, which means a clandestine group of sympathizers who infiltrate enemy lines for the purpose of undermining the enemy. Franco stated that his four army column would attack Madrid from the outside, while his Fifth Column trusted followers would attack from the inside, employing the tactics of espionage and sabotage.

Later, these same tactics were applied by pro-Nazi minorities living throughout Europe. One of the regions was Poland, where the Nazi minority developed and skillfully implemented their spy networks in southern Poland. The location was very useful for the movement. One of the spiritual leaders and Nazi minority organizers was engineer and architect Rudolph Wiesner, an Austrian. He was a staunch supporter of Hitler's ideology. In 1921, Wiesner founded in Bielsko Biala, Poland an organization identified as Detsher Nationalsozialistisher Vrein Fur Polen, the forerunner of what was to become in 1930 the Jungdeutsche Partei (Young Nazi Party). This party was deeply brainwashed by Hitler ideology.

After World War I, Nazi minorities living in Poland were not paying attention to Hitler's ideology until Hitler became chancellor of Germany. Then, drastic changes took place in the minds of Nazi minorities, particularly in the minds of young Nazi Party members who preached the ideology based on two writings: The DerAufbruch and Deuthsche Nachrichtn. Shortly thereafter, the Wiesnera Party became very active promulgating Hitler's ideology in southern Poland. The Yungdeutsche Partei tried very hard to become the monopoly among Nazi minorities. They fought smaller and more moderate parties in the Nazi organizations. They particularly counted on young people trying new methods to bring in new members.

The political climate was more favorable to Wiesner after the signing of the non-aggression pact between Germany and Poland on January 26, 1934. Hitler's followers found the conditions more conducive to expanding their movement in the spirit of National Socialism. Shortly after, Wiesner, with his political ambitions, was appointed a member of the senate by Polish President Ignacy Moscicki, where he represented Nazi minorities who lived in Poland.

As a senator, he was immune from any intimidation and any investigation. He took the opportunity to organize mass meetings of Nazi minorities, which had anti-Polish characters.

One of the meetings took place in 1935, on the anniversary of returning parts of Polish western lands to Germany. This persuaded Wiesner that the remaining disputed land would be returned to Germany and its citizens would come under Hitler's wing. The deep political changes took place in southern Poland at the foot of the Carpathian Mountains, as the Nazi minorities flourished in Bielsko Biala and surrounding areas. Bielsko Biala's nickname was Little Berlin, and Wiesner was the master of the region. His technical and administrative personnel were chosen from Nazi minorities. When Wiesner had a shortage of skillful people, he turned his request to Berlin. Berlin responded by sending Nazis to his area. The Polish authority issued visas to Nazis without performing background checks. Later, these same Nazis extended their visas, and were the ideal spies for Nazi headquarters in Berlin. Almost all Nazi minority organizations were inspired by Berlin. They kept in communication with Berlin and trained their members in special units. Some members received their training in Berlin with Hitler. During one of the meetings in 1934, Hitler told them,

> "On you, rests the most important movement in our cause. We should guard our Nazi existence. You should create attacking divisions; therefore you will be active in not what everyone believes, but follow and listen winning commands. This may seem to be beneficial as a an upper point of vision but may be damaging. Therefore, I require from you blind listening. It is not your duty to make decisions about what to do in your regions. I can't always tell you what is in the details of what my plan is. You are at the frontiers of Nazism, in the first line in our fight and will help begin our march

forward and it will begin the activities of war. You are the guards. You have to make certain tasks and work long before our front begins. You must prepare for an attack. You have the obligation of the war laws; you are the most important part of the Nazi nation."

From Hitler's encouragement, the Nazis flourished in Poland. The vision fulfilled the mission of the Third Reich, particularly the National Socialist interests that had great support from the Nazi organization in Germany. One of the major foundations was the Deutsche Stifung (Nazi Foundation) which was financially supported by private enterprise. Active outside of Germany, among major supporters in Poland, was Auslands Organizationder NSDAP, which was created first in May 1931, and directed by Ernesta Whilhema Bohle. In 1933, this organization issued a directive to all Nazis living outside of Germany to admit openly that they were Nazis. Hitler's success in international areas, like the victory of General Franco in Spain and the Monahium occupation of Austria and part of Czechoslovakia, encouraged the Nazi minorities in Poland to expand their cause in spreading Hitler's ideology. They were persuaded that all disputed land between Poland and Germany would be returned to the Third Reich.

The most active in the movement was the Young Nazi Party, under the leadership of Rudolph Wiesner. Wiesner's party in 1930 had only 300 members, but grew to 50,000 just before the advent of World War II. Members were spread throughout Poland. Many had special training in Berlin for purposes of spying on Poland. They were very close to Nazi spy intelligence in Germany. Members worked in Poland as specialists, factory workers and in many institutions. They developed spy intelligence networks at recreation facilities at the foot of the Carpathian Mountains. The Nazis held spy meetings at many of the tourist areas, and conducted young party training for future spies. All the activities were directed by the Nazi military intelligence agency. They were more aggressive and took a more active part in April 1939 when Hitler broke the non-aggression pact with Poland. Wiesner immediately organized units and prepared to fight under the Freikorps, whose purposes was to lay the groundwork for the Nazi army in the first days of the war. All covert operations under the propaganda umbrella which announced that Nazi minorities were being discriminated. The Nazis, under covert operations and in an attempt to create a scapegoat, blew up their own office buildings, schools and private houses. They even went so far as to destroy the statue of Schillera and the statues of Nazis who died during World War I.

One purpose of the Nazi covert operation before actual military occupation in Poland was to protect and secure all important buildings, strategic industries, bridges, roads, and railroad networks. It was essential to the Nazi military machine that Polish factories were available to them for use once the occupation was complete. The Nazi organization Abweha was formed to protect the factories. Nazis had plans for immediate production of weapons and warfare equipment. All these plans were in force in the spring 1939, and in July, more than 4,400 people conducted such covert operations.

In 1939, Bielsko Biala, Poland was an island of Nazi language. The Young Nazi party members held key positions in Polish institutions and police departments. The used their positions to spy on Polish citizens. Freikorps, Hilfspolizei, Selbstschutz were the precursors to the Gestapo, who waited in the wings. Some Nazis who conspired with the Polish authorities left Poland. However, they later either returned with the Nazi army, or they were sent to the backlines of the Polish army for the purpose of spreading propaganda and chaos, which eventually laid the groundwork for Nazis to operate on land and in the air.

The covert operation was very well developed in the Beskidy Mountains. All the tourist attractions were the point of contact for and spies networking for destruction and sabotage. All Nazi groups were supplied with weapons through the Third Reich. Because the region was close to Czechoslovakia and the terrain was easily traversed, it gave Nazis excellent conditions for smuggling guns across the border. Some weapons smuggling took place through trade and business contacts. It could be said that Nazi minorities in the foothills were very well prepared to execute tasks given to them by Berlin. From the other side, however, Polish authorities and civilians undermined many Nazi actions with less than favorable outcomes. Even armed with good information, the Polish undercover agency was not able to react against the Nazi organization because of governmental bureaucracy.

One of the leaders, General Joseph Kustron, in a November 1937 memorandum to Polish Marshal Edward Smiglego, warned about the danger from Nazis. In his memorandum, he also stated that Rudolph Wiesner should be dismissed from the Senate because of his role against Poland in the Youngdeutsche Party, and that they were undermining Polish security. It was well documented that Nazi minorities were trained as missionaries to spy on Poland. Additionally, Nazi politicians expressed entitlement to own part of Poland, and they acted like magnets on Polish territory.

The Polish military compromised and uncovered many spies connected with Freikorpsem. In many cases, the military's cooperation with the local citizenry in the mountain region led them to uncover many spies and Nazi actions. The Polish army intelligence was able to discover many secret Nazi hiding places, but they were not able to win the undercover operation directed by Fifth Column. Poland paid heavily in the beginning of the war.

Fearing the Nazi occupation and the threats to be killed, most villagers decided to leave their homes and small farms. Once quiet, narrow, graveled village roads were transformed into an unending procession. Each hour, the waves of refugees grew, creating one human chain, separated by caravans, the bawling of their livestock echoing across the valley. News of the imminent Nazi invasion spilled into the most remote eastern mountain villages, with the courier who sped along urging the settlers to leave their homes.

Waves of refugees were approaching the small town of Bystra, the shortest route to other side of the mountains. There were a few scattered houses in the upper part of the village. Several hundred feet away from the uphill road lived Michal, a very prosperous farmer, his second wife Neska, and three children. Michal's farm stretched alongside both sides of the Juszczynka River. From the banks of the river, prime farmland stretched three hundred feet to the south side hill. The open field gave a spectacular view of the western mountains.

It was afternoon, first September in 1939. Michal was working in his large barn. The attached stable smelled of hay and manure. Stored in the loft overhead was the hay. It was easy to pitch down to the cows and horses below through the small opening in the stable ceiling. On the opposite side of the loft was a large storage area for straw. The barn was warm in winter when the animals stayed indoors. During the summer days, the barn doors stood wide open to capture the cooling breeze.

Michal pitched his last harvested straw onto the second floor of the storage bin. Taking a short break from his work, he wiped the perspiration from his face, using the right arm of his long-sleeved shirt. Then he heard the echoes of the refugees. Michal dropped his pitchfork, ran into his house, and found his wife taking a nap. His thirteen-year-old daughter Maria was taking care of her four-year-old brother and eight-year old sister Hanka.

Seeing the look on her father's face, Maria ran to Michal. "Tata, what happened?" Maria asked. Michal looked out at the road through the window and saw the first caravans passing. Waves of people were following behind. The dry, sunny weather churned up dustbowls along the gravel road. For a while, Michal observed the tragedy of the long human chain walking towards the east. He held Maria under his arm and whispered, barely moving his lips. He moved his head from side to side in disbelief because he had never seen such a crowd of people. Michal sat on old chair near his stove, slumped his shoulders, bent his head toward his knees, and buried his face in his palms. "Tata, what happened? Why are you so sad?" Maria asked.

"Oh, my child, you may never know," Michal said.

Dust from the road quickly settled over the house windows, masking the once clear view of the road. Michal arose from his chair and looked towards the window. He did not see the two men running down the hill behind his house. Coming around to the front porch, they knocked hard on the door. "Open the door! Open the door!" one man yelled.

Michal opened the door. "What do you want?"

The man said, "The Nazis are rounding up all the men for the Nazi army. You must be ready to leave your home, to save your family. If you do not believe us, then come to the road. See the waves of refugees escaping from the western front? I do not lie to you. Everyone is leaving. You must go."

"No, I do not want to go," Michal said. "No, I have my children, and who is going to take care of my home and my cows and the rest of the livestock?"

"You are going to be killed if you stay," the second man yelled. "You are crazy to stay!" He pushed the door against Michal's face. With faces twisted in anger and disbelief, the men ran to the next neighbor to report the Nazi invasion.

Michal paced around the room, back and forth, back and forth. He peered again through the grimy window, considering what he should do. "Do I stay here, or not?" he repeated aloud several times. Pausing for a moment, he then asked his children and his wife to wait for him. "I will be back, he said.

"Can I want to go with you, Tata?" Maria asked.

"No," Michal said. "You stay here."

Michal left, walking behind his house to the narrow path that was a shortcut to the road. He climbed the hill to the road and stopped in front of the huge oak tree, its branches leaning over the hill and bordering the road. He watched the throngs of people trudging towards the mountains to the east. He saw wagons pass, carrying their cargo of elderly women wrapped in scarves, holding small children on their laps. At the end of the wagons were cows tied with rope to their horns. Young boys swung their sweeps behind the animals, pretending to hit them.

For a moment, Michal turned his head toward his farm. Suddenly he heard loud voices as he was nearly hit by the caravan. "Come with us! Come with us! Do not stay here. The Nazis are going to take you to the army. They will kill your family!"

Filled with fear now for the first time, Michal walked slowly to his home, his mind racing. "What I am going to do with my children? Can I safely take them across the rough terrain of the mountain forests? What happens when winter arrives?"

Back in the stable, Michal opened two small windows to let in more fresh air. His two horses turned their heads toward Michal. His cows stood in opposite rows; his chickens, now disturbed, flew from their nests. Michal lifted the two leather bridles from their hooks on the wall, fitted them on the horses' necks, swung open the gate, and walked the animals to a wagon near the shelter.

The shelter was little more than a tiny shed that protected his wagons, ladders, pitchforks, and other farm equipment. He harnessed the horses to the wagon and tied their bridles to the hook on the shed wall. Michal did not want the horses wandering away while he continued his work. Returning to the stable for the cows, he found the long woolen rope hanging on the swing gate. He tied the rope to the cows' horns, led the animals to the rear of the wagon, and secured them to the back.

In no hurry, Michal returned sadly to house. "Maria, take Stas and dress him warmly. Hanka and Neska, we must go. Take the pillows and the rest of the food and the kerosene lamp. Maria, do not forget your blankets. Neska, please take the basket and bread."

Maria gathered the child and Mother Neska, and led them to the front door. "Wait for me here," Michal instructed them.

Michal discarded the potato bags and swept the dirt from the wagon. Several bales of hay spread across the bottom would make the ride more comfortable. He brought the wagon to the front of the house. Maria and Neska carried all their belongings outside and carefully stacked them on the cart that would be their means of escape. Neska lifted Stas and put him next to their things, covering him with hay to keep him warm.

Returning to the barn, Michal climbed the old ladder into the attic, found two bags of grain, threw them on his back, and stacked them next to the front seat of the wagon. His family was now prepared to leave their home. Michal locked the house with two big locks and hid the key under the large stone by the front porch.

Michal loosened the bridle reins and started the horses up the hilly driveway. The muscular animals strained to pull the wagon to the shoulder of the narrow road.

"Per, Per," Michal called for horses to stop as he waited for the convoy of refugees to pass.

Behind the convoy, Michal saw two Polish military officers marching towards him. He waited for them, and then interrupted their march by taking off his hat off from his head, and waving with his right hand. "Good afternoon," Michal called to them.

"Good afternoon," the men said, the buttons on their uniforms reflecting the sun's light.

"Sir, where do I take my children?" Michal asked. "Where should we go? Please advise me what to do."

One of the officers looked around the wagon. He saw Maria sitting on the end of wagon wrapped in her warm fall cloth, and he gently caressed her face. He looked at Stas nestled in the hay in the middle of the wagon, sitting like a helpless baby bird. "You must turn around and go back home," the officer said. "Take care of your children and stay home."

"But the Nazis will….." Michal could not finish his sentence. "What will happen to my children and my home when the Nazis come?"

"Listen, Sir," the officer continued, "if you follow the crowd of refugees, you do not know what will happen. There is no safe haven anywhere, not in the east side of the mountains. The Nazis will be there soon. I do not think they will harm you. Just stay home. As soldiers and officers, we must follow our orders to join the units and regroup."

"Thank you, thank you." Michal grabbed the officer's hand, bent his head, and repeated again, "Thank you."

The officer hid his tears as he walked away. Michal stepped in front of his horses, took a firm hold of their bridles, and pushed while whispering, "Go back. Go back. Easy, easy."

Responding to his command, the horses cautiously plodded backward, pushing the wagon into the small grassy field, barely missing the deep ditch. Michal turned the horses' heads and started them on the narrow road that led downhill to his home.

Michal parked the wagon at the corner of the house, unhitched the horses from the family wagon, and walked them to the stable. He returned for his cows and walked them to the stable as well. From the loft, he threw down several bales of hay for his livestock. He double locked the stable and barn, and returned to his house where his small family waited.

It was late afternoon. The sunset brushed the mountain peaks with deep colors, casting long shadows and signaling nightfall. Fear of the impending Nazi invasion continued to bombard Michal's head. He returned to his barn and checked to be sure the doors were closed. To reassure himself that nothing strange was going on, he looked around few more times. Before returning home, he stopped at the front of the high stack of firewood under the barn roof, and placed into his right arm several logs of the firewood, and carried them to the house.

As he entered the porch, Maria heard his steps on the wooden floor and opened the door for him. He placed the wood near brick stove at the left corner of the room, the place used for cooking and baking. The smaller iron stove at the center wall was used during the fall and winter seasons to heat the bedroom and living room.

With the sunset, the sky turned into red and orange stripes, hanging over the mountain horizon. Then slowly red and orange disappeared, shortly followed by gray scattered clouds steadily flowing over the valley bringing nightfall. Michal lit the kerosene lamp and hung it at the center of the ceiling. The light from the lamp was sufficient to see the entire room, and partially illuminated the bedroom across the open door as the light broke through the curtain hung over the door. "Tata, when are you going to make a fire in the stove? I want you to make fire. I want to see the fire," Stas said.

"Come here, Stas," Michal said as he pulled the small chair closer to the stove. "Sit here." As Stas sat on his chair and Michal built the fire, Maria went out of the room to the storage near the porch and collected in her basket of large potatoes.

She returned to the room and placed the basket near the stove. "I will bake these potatoes for our supper," she said turning to Neska and her sister Hanka.

After the stove warmed up and the wood started to burn and turn into red charcoal, Michal opened the stove door. "Maria, give me these potatoes."

"Yes Tata," she replied, and gave him the basket with full of big potatoes.

One by one, he threw the potatoes over the red ashes under the hot grid. The potato skins quickly turned black as the ashes were falling over them. "Watch the potatoes, Maria."

Five minutes later, Maria opened the stove door and with a long wooden stick she turned them over, being careful not to let them burn. After another five minutes, she grabbed another sharp stick and punched each potato to check if they were already baked. The potatoes looked like solid charcoal as Maria collected them from the stove and dropped them into the basket. As Stas tried to reach for one of the hot potatoes Maria shouted to him, "Stas, do not pick them up!" But it was too late as he burned his fingers when he grabbed one, and quickly dropped the potato on the floor. He started to cry. Neska took some butter, which served as medicine, and rubbed it on his fingers. "You will be well soon," she said, as the butter melted over his burned fingers.

As Stas licked the warm butter off of his fingers, he said, "Tata, I will be fine," showing his hands to his father and sitting next to him. After Maria collected all the potatoes from the hot stove, she cleaned them from the charcoal using a small rough sand rock. As the potato skins turned brown, and the black dust settled over her hands, Maria placed them on the table while Michal cut some bacon and set out the butter and salt.

Michal's family had their traditional supper at least once a month. The tradition was long-standing, and the whole family always eagerly anticipated the occasion. The evening slowly ended when the stove burned the last piece of firewood and the fire crackling stopped. Michal pulled down the knob of kerosene lamp, and everyone went to sleep.

On September 1, 1939 at 5:45 a.m., the first telegraph arrived at the main army defense headquarters announcing that Germany had attacked southern Poland. The information arrived through an army officer in Krakow. The Nazis are attacking with heavy artillery, airplanes, and manpower. The villagers who decided to remain stood on the hillside watching with fear as huge fires erupted, belching thick clouds of smoke. On the morning of September 2, the Nazis attacked from each direction in Poland's southern mountain region. With weak defense lines facing them in the foothill villages, the swollen Nazi army faced little to no resistance from the Poles.

After the sweeping first victories, the Nazi army was confident that the entire region held no further obstacles, and that the Polish resistance had given up. The Nazi army moved quickly through the small, mostly deserted mountain villages, encountering only sporadic resistance from the partisans who were taking potshots from the forest. It was mostly young men who ran to the forest during the first battles with the Nazi army, and somehow, they managed to avoid the open fields which were teeming with Nazi soldiers.

Then early in the morning on September 2, 1939, the Nazi army entered a suburb of the small town, Wegierska Gorka, and unexpectedly encountered heavy resistance coming from the forts between the mountain ridges. The region was one of the most important fortified areas in the South of Poland during the Defensive War in 1939. The stronghold was complex of fortification; built shortly before the outbreak of the Second World War. Its purpose was to defend the strategically important road and railway line in the valley to east of Poland. Nazi artillery divisions used airplanes to attack the forts, and shelled them until late afternoon when the infantry division took over the attack.

The forts fought bravely as the Nazi casualties grew. The Nazi command sent their best division to crush the defense lines and forcibly take the foothills of the corridor. At the slopes of the edge of the forest mountain, in the last oldest built bunker suranded by ditches and bulks of large rocks, gave the soldiers more confidence of repeal the Nazi attacks. The soldiers kept their defence line not realized that the Nazi took over the foothills. From the bunker, the soldiers kept shooting at the Nazis and held their positions, using several heavy machine guns and two small cannons, five soldiers sat on small, circular shaped, fully movable chairs attached to an iron post. The chairs were set next to narrow (10 x 16 inch) windows. The barrels of the machine guns were two feet outside of the windows, and the soldiers kept their fingers on the triggers. At the same time, the other soldiers were busy bringing in more ammunition from the back of the bunker, which they quickly helped to reload.

The Nazis charged under the fire of heavy artillery, and tried to capture the bunker. "I got them, I got them!" the soldiers called out from each side of the bunker window as the Nazis fell to the ground. The Nazis kept charging until some got to the foot of the bunker and communicated to their unit to stop shooting. The Nazis stopped shooting as soon as they saw their troops reach the bunkers from other side. The Nazis dropped several grenades through the small, narrow windows. As the grenades exploded near the passages to other rooms, the hallways became black with smoke. One soldier was hit on his chest. He called for help. The others pulled him away from the hallway as he was choking from the smoke, and leaned him against the wall. They gave him first aid to address his wounds, but the bleeding could not be stopped. Shortly after, he was declared dead.

Then the Nazis stopped shooting at the bunker. There was silence as the soldiers changed position and reloaded their guns with the remaining ammunition. The Nazis sneaked behind the banker, threw more graneds into the bunker, attached heavy explosives into the bunker walls, and then ran away, pulling cables away from the bunker and hiding behind ditches. They ignited a battery, which exploded and crashed part of the concrete wall. As the stones flew into the air and away from the bunker, the surface was exposed, revealing iron bars. However, the thick concrete reinforced walls stand strong.

After the explosions, one soldier rushed into the back room where there was an exit to the roof, with a machine gun installed. He saw Nazis running in the fields, he fired at them and watched as several dropped at the ground. The Nazis withdrew behind the artillery line and shelled the bunker, the soldier quickly slid inside to avoid being shot.

The Nazis regrouped and rearmed, this time with flamethrowers. The soldiers fought until their machine gun barrels were overheated and could no longer could used. The commander inside one bunker called to the soldiers, "We must give up," and gave instructions to the corporal to raise the white flag of surrender. As the corporal stepped out of the bunker, waving the small white flag, the Nazis stopped shooting. They waited as one–by–one the soldiers left the bunker. There were only eight remaining, and the Nazis could not believe that those eight men fought so bravely. The Nazis angrily marched towards the soldiers and kicked them until they fell to the ground. They then went about their business of collecting the Nazi dead and wounded soldiers.

On the other side of the side of mountain, the other trenches defended their post until nightfall, when they were able to move under cover of darkness.

Even at night, they were fired upon. The shells lit up the night sky. Some landed near the bunkers and trenches crashing into the observation posts. The debris containing large log fragments flew in all directions, sometimes hitting the soldiers on their heads as they were crouched in the trenches. Several wounded soldiers screamed for help.

The only way the nurses could locate them in the dark was by following the sounds of screaming. Those soldiers who found themselves under the log debris could not move because they were trapped underneath by the weight of the logs.

Although the nurses could touch the wounded soldiers' shoulders, they had difficulty pulling them from the ruins of the trenches. They would reach the soldiers' hands, remove the wood, pull them to the edge of the trench, lay them over the stretchers, lift them, and run towards the thick woods, then entering the hidden underground shelter covered with sod and pine branches. They moved the wounded soldiers inside the shelter, placing them near the candles' light. In darkness of the night, the nurses returned quickly to the trenches hoping to save other soldiers' lives. They could barely see, it did not matter because they knew the territory well. The other soldiers laying inside on the field beds watched the wounded soldiers when the one nurse gave the soldiers first aid, wrapped them in blankets, laid them near them, and then quickly returned to the posts to aid other wounded fighters. The Nazis attacked throughout the night and continued shelling until the following day when their forces advanced towards the east.

Michal woke up earlier, and slowly stepped towards the window and slightly moved towards the curtain as the daylight barely began. Although it was still dark outside, he had a clear view of the road. It was silent, and no trace was left behind showing the refugees leaving the village. Michal closed the curtain and lit the kerosene lamp, placing it against the opposite wall away from children's bedroom. Very carefully, he opened the stove door and built a fire from the scrap of dried wood stored in the corner. He pulled his favorite rocking chair nearer to the stove and dropped several wood chips inside the stove. As the heat from the stove was quickly warming up the entire room, Michal rocked back and forth, closed his eyes, and took an early morning nap.

As the first daylight broke through the curtain window and a small convoy of motorcycles roared towards the east through the village road, the sound woke up Michal. He jumped from the chair, splashed his face with cold water, and rushed towards the window. He caught a glimpse of jeeps with large Polish flags moving very fast towards the east of the mountains. Michal quietly walked to the hallway and slowly closed the door behind him, being careful not to wake up the family. As he stepped outside and started to walk to the end of the porch to get better view of the east side of the road, he began to shiver as the chilly fall morning wind landed on his shoulders.

He grabbed his working coat from the hanger outside of the porch door and dropped it over his arms. From the porch, Michal looked at the rising sun above the mountain horizon. He looked towards the blue, clear sky and raised his hands up and prayed, I must do whatever it takes to protect my family and my livelihood." Then he placed his hands on the top of the porch rails, kneeled, but he he was interrupted by the whine of airplane engines from above. He stopped his prayers to see where the noise was coming from, and saw two airplanes from the west flying low over the hills. It seemed that they were chasing the columns just passing by, but they turned around.

The planes turned sharply in circles above Michal's fields. He was temporarily blinded when the sun reflected off the wings, shining directly into his face. He shaded his eyes to block the sun, and looked up. He recognized the planes as being Nazi. He briefly saw black, twisted crosses painted on the wings. The planes were flying fast, dropping leaflets all over his fields and the deserted village. They quickly disappeared behind the mountains range, leaving behind long streams of dark smoke. As the planes were leaving the fields and dropped leaflets behind them, several gunshots rang out from the forest. The leaflets were lying over the field, and the wind blew them closer to home, landing between the barn and stable, and over the courtyard. Some hung over the rooftops, and some blew away from the front of the house.

Michal lifted a few of the leaflets from the ground. As he was ready to toss them, he saw a swastika on the letterhead and orders written in large letters, easy to read in the Polish language. He slowly red the message. "The Nazi Army is not fighting against peaceful citizens and people without arms. Work as usual and do not take any action against Nazis. Whoever takes any action against the Nazi Army and aids the resistance, or whoever hides weapons and explosives will be punished according to the laws of the war. The Nazi Army guarantees peaceful citizen's safety. People who will be attacking Nazi soldiers will be severely punished. Additionally, from sunset to sunrise, dark blankets shall cover the lights in the house. All village residents should stay around their homes."

As he finished his reading, Michal remembered that the officer was right, the officer was right. He repeated that many times. As he was about to go into the house, he saw from a distance, alongside the forest line, two men approaching the house. As they got closer to house, Michal was glad that they were not Nazis. They were clothed in long green coats, unshaved, and very tired looking, with rifles slung on their shoulders. As they passed, holding firmly to their guns, they waved to Michal using a small Polish flag, and called out to him, "We need food and supplies. We are partisan fighters. We have little time to catch up with others."

"Please wait here. I will bring you some dried meat and a loaf of bread, but you must leave my farm," Michal said, as he looked at the leaflets scattered on the ground to read. Michal became very angry as he remembered reading one leaflet message in particular, "Aiding and helping partisans, and resistance to Nazis is punishable by death."

These beasts, he thought.

Michal ran quickly to the house and found that all his family was awake. "Tata, Tata," Stas cried out as he ran towards his nervous father.

Hanka stopped Stas and pulled him to a bed in the kitchen.

"Michal, what is going on?" she nervously asked him.

"Nothing. Please, give me the two loaves of the bread and some smoked meat." Michal was in a hurry, and could not wait around to explain. He grabbed the bread off the table, snatched the meat hanging above the oven, wrapped it with white cloth, dropped them both in a brown paper sack, and rushed back outside to the partisans. "Here," he said. "I brought you some food," and gave it to them.

One of the partisans slung his weapon alongside the bag of food. "Thank you, we may return for more." Then the group of partisans left, walking towards the other side of the thick forest.

Michal, recalling the warnings on the leaflets, quickly returned to house. He climbed the wooden, squeaking steps to the attic where he found old black blankets stored inside an equally old, dusty wooden box. He pulled the blankets out of the box and slid them towards the porch steps. They were covered with dust and smelled stale from sitting in the attic, so he hung the blanket over the porch railing. "Maria," he called out, "bring me the broom."

"Yes, Tata, I will be there," she called as she pulled the broom from under the kitchen sink. "Tata, I want to help you to clean the blankets," she said as she brushed the blankets and struck them hard several times in order to dislodge the dirt and dust. When she was done, Maria left them on the railing to air out in the mild wind.

Michal, believing that the Nazis would not harm him, decided that this was the perfect time for him and Maria to harvest the remaining cabbages, and clean the fields. Although it was fall, the weather was sunny and warm – what the villagers called old women summer. Maria and Michal harvested the remaining cabbages, cleaned the fields of the dried potato vines, gathered the vines together in the middle of the field and burned them. The rising smoke partially covered the field.

Everyone in the village recognized the smell of the smoke as dried potato vines, as well as the partisans who were hiding in the forest. The partisans did not come to Michal's farm. Neska, Hanka, and the boy stayed home, working in the kitchen and preparing lunch. Michal and Maria, after working all morning in the fields, returned home for lunch as they heard Neska call for them. The valley echoed back Neska's words, "Lunch is ready."

Michal carried some fresh potatoes in old basket on his back. "Tata, when we finish our lunch, will we be cleaning the rest of the dried potatoes vines?" Maria asked.

"Yes, but we must also collect all the cabbage, and tomorrow we will have to clean the field." Entering the house through the porch, Michal tapped his shoes against the stone. The dirt fell under the steps.

The table was ready when Stas said, "Tata, I will eat with you," as he sat close to Michal's chair.

After lunch, the entire family went back out to work in the fields. Hanka and Stas walked around the edge of the harvested field while Neska put the dried vines in the center. Maria put some cabbages at the small wheel barrow, and pushed it towards the large wagon with the horse patiently waiting at the end of the field.

It was late afternoon, when Maria with the wheelbarrow approached the wagon, and was ready to toss the cabbages inside; suddenly a loud explosion behind the hills startled her. The horse, also startled, tossed his feedbag over his head. Fortunately, he was tethered to the tree. Maria dropped the wheelbarrow from her hands, and the cabbage fell all over the ground near the wagon. Michal on the other end of the field yelled loudly, "Mary, Maria! Neska, take Stas and Hanka and run to house, run to house."

Mary, at the last moment, grabbed one cabbage in her hand and ran quickly, straight to the house. Out of breath, she fell on the front porch floor to catch her breath. Michal left much of his work in the field, and rushed to bring the other horse and cows pastured near the forest line into the stable. He left them a bale of hay for their feed for the rest of the day. He locked the stable door and rechecked the barn to make certain everything was closed. As he walked around the barn, he heard several more explosions coming from behind the mountains. He saw heavy, dark smoke slowly mixed with clouds rising behind the hills, covering the covered the sunset, just touching the mountainside.

It was at that moment Michal realized that the Nazis were fast approaching, and he must follow the orders from the Nazis' leaflets to cover the windows of his house after dusk. Shortly after dusk, Michal went to pick up the blankets from the porch, and dropped them at the center of the living room.

"Maria, please bring the hammer and small nails from the storage while Neska builds the fire in wood stove," Michal said. He carefully measured the length of the blankets and the window widths to see if the blankets would fit. He pushed small table against the wall with the window and climbed on the chair, holding one end of the blanket. Maria, while holding several nails in one hand, passed the hammer to her father. Michal carefully nailed the end of the blanket onto the upper corner of the window edge, spread the blanket across, and nailed it to other, upper corner of the window. "Neska, go get the other kerosene lamp," Michal told her. From the bedroom, Neska brought another kerosene lamp, lit it, and hung it over the stove. Stas sat on the small carpet and played with small wooden blocks with his sister, as he had done on many other days.

Michal tied the blanket below the edge of the window and carefully nailed it again. He checked every open space between the edges of the window, and additionally stretched the blanket all around the edge, making sure there were no gaps. He stepped outside to make sure that no light was visible from the outside. Just to make sure, he walked over the hill and up the road from above the house. From near distance, he knelt down and carefully looked at the window if there is any sight of the light. He saw only the dark house and other buildings off to the side, he rechecked them, walked around the stable and peeped through the small stable windows where the chickens were kept at night. The animals felt his presence and the cows mooed, and the clouds opened the sky revealing a full moon illuminating the entire court. For a moment, Michal stopped under the clear sky, watched the stars, and looked at the reflected moon from the river. It was very quiet late in the evening, with only the sound of the river and hunting owls, which he was used to hearing in his daily life.

As the evening was passing quietly, Neska prepared a light supper: some scrambled eggs with bacon and coffee, with a little sugar. The supper was short. Michal asked all his family to pray, and to kneel in front of the wooden carved cross hung above the kitchen table wall. As the family kneeled in the front of the cross, Micha asked his family to follow him, saying his prayers, "Our Father, thank you for what you have already given to us. Our Father, you are indivisible. You gave us your existence. Our Father, please save us from the dangerous world. Please safeguard our home.

After the prayer, Stas run towards Michael and gave him a hug and Anka held her hands on Michal's shoulder. "Go sleep, my children, you going to be fine, as he tied his lips" and controlled his emotions and hold his tears inside him.

From the fear of danger of death, Neska look for her salvation kept clutching her rosary moving the beads quickly in her hand as Maria stepped out from her side and dropped more wood into the iron stove to keep the fire in as Michal turned down the kerosene knob and went to his bed in the kitchen. Instead of going to bed, Maria lay down on the sheepskin on the floor near the stove and watched the fire. The flames cast shadows, which escaped from the cracks of the stove door and danced against the white front wall. She listened to the crackling of the sparks until she fell asleep.

Late evening on September 3, 1939, the Polish stronghold fell at the hands of the Nazi Seventh Army, Bavarian Division. The remaining single group of Polish soldiers with light arms retreated into the East and deep mountain forests. The battle delayed the Nazi advancement on the eastern front, and they were ordered by the high command to move in a hurry.

The Nazi Army quickly moved their troops across the mountain roads, until they reached Bystra village. They drove in light trucks, with attached cannons at the back of the line with a battalion of soldiers marching behind. The Nazi commanding officer drove on a motorcycle sidecar from behind the column of soldiers and passed them as he reached the first group. He stopped in front of them. "Halt," he said to the first group, "we will camp near the farmer's house." An officer directed the convoy to Michal's farm. The soldiers briefly aimed their bright lights at Michal's house and his fields. They saw a perfect site to camp. From the dirt road, the convoys drove down to the Michal's farm. The Nazi officers directed that the convoy must camp near the river. They crossed between the barns and the house. The officers reminded the soldiers not to disturb anyone in the house. With the help of the moonshine, they knew that someone was in the house, when they observed that smoke was rising from the house's chimney.

At the house, the fire continued to burn in the stove as Maria slept soundly on the sheepskin covered by a small, light blanket. As the Nazis entered the courtyard and walked near the house, the noise woke up Michal. He heard noises behind outside, lit his kerosene lamp, and very carefully walked around the room. Then he placed the lamp on the kitchen table and looked at the grandfather clock on the kitchen wall. It was nine o'clock. The noise he made walking around woke up Maria. She sprang up from the floor. Michal whispered to her, "Ci, Ci, come over here."

"Tata, I hear someone outside. Who are these people?"

"Don't worry, don't worry," Michal said as he hugged her. "All right. It will be all right," Michal told her. Again, Michal looked at the grandfather clock. Time seemed to stand still. It appeared to him that the hands on the clock were not moving.

Michael stoked the fire, adding more logs to keep it burning. Neska woke up, threw her legs over the side of the bed, quickly took her rosary from the night table near the bed, and started to pray with the hope that no one would knock on the door.

The living room became silent as Michal heard the horses neighing in the stable. He whispered to Maria and Neska to be quiet. He saw people running outside the house. At first, he thought that there were other partisans, but then he pressed his ear on blanket covering the window and heard the men speaking German. He immediately turned off the kerosene lamp, and lit two candles, placing them at the corner site away from the window side. Maria clung to Michal's arms. "Tata, who are these people? Why they come to our farm? Are they going to take us with them?"

"No, no," Michal assured her. Stas started to cry, and the younger sister tried to calm him down, but he cried even more.

"Hanka, please take care of him and make him stop crying," Neska said. Hanka took Stas in her hands and was able to calm him down and get him to sleep.

The Nazis outside were loudly yelling, "Schnell, schnell!"

He was worried that they would come into the house, but they didn't. They did, however, go to the barns, and broke open the locks using the butts of their guns. They pitched most of the straw outside, and used it as bedding at their campsite. "Maria," Michal asked, "sit here close to the stove and please be quiet. I will climb to the attic to see what is going on in the field." Stas and Hanka were sleeping.

Neska got up from the bed nearby and grabbed the small iron cross from the wall. She sat back at the corner of the bed closer to window, held the cross to her chest, kissed it twice, and prayed silently, never moving her lips. In the dark, she looked like a ghost. In her panic, all the color was drained from her face. She continued to hold the cross while the Nazi soldier tripped over a stack of wooden logs near the window; the crack made a loud noise, Neska got very frightened and walked away from the window site and walked to other room where Hanka and Stas were sleeping. Maria slowly on her toes walked to the window and placed her ear to the blanket over the glass then found a small opening at the corner, she peeped through as one Nazi soldier passed the window side. Maria with her fear that he saw her quickly bounced back from the window and sat over the bed and waited for her father.

In darkness, Michal very carefully climbed over the squealing attic steps, and slowly opened the heavy door overhead. He was careful not to let the Nazis know that someone was awake in the house. He held the rail, which guided him in the attic, and slowly tiptoed to the other side. He knelt over the truss and peeked through small cracks, hoping that the moonlight would allow him to see into his field where the Nazis were encamped.

The soldiers were working hard spreading the straw. Several soldiers were talking loudly as they approached the house. Although Michal could hear them, he was having trouble understanding them. He went to the other side of the attic to get a different view of the barn. Michal saw that the barn door was wide open. All the straw he had harvested for the winter to feed his livestock was strew everywhere. He pressed his forehead and both hands against the board. *What are they doing to me? What are they doing to my family? This was my harvest for winter. What I am going to do?* At that moment, one of the soldiers yelled, "Stop, stop!" and then he yelled stop several more times.

The moonlight lasted only a short time longer. Soon the dark clouds covered the valley and brought darkness to the attic. Michal hoped that the cloud would move away again. For a moment, he waited as he heard more Nazi troops move around his barn. He was worried that the family would wake up. When it was dark, he slowly made his way back to the living room, then turned towards the bedroom where he saw Neska, Hanka, and Stas sleeping soundly. "Tato, are we safe?" Maria softly asked.

"Yes, we are safe, go back to sleep," he said and placed the other pillow near her side. "Go to sleep my child we will be fine." Confident that the Nazis were going to leave his family alone, an exhausted Michal fell into couch.

The next morning, Michal woke up, and immediately rushed to the blacked-out window and carefully pulled back a corner of the blanket. He saw a large Nazi motorized convoy followed by horses. Then from the corner of the house, he saw many soldiers walking on the road. "Oh, oh," he breathed heavily. With disbelief, he said out loud, "They left me alone. They left my family alone."

As Maria woke up and heard him, she quickly stepped from her bed calling, "Tata, Tata, what happened? Who is there?"

Michal said, "Go back to sleep, go back to bed."

"No, no," Maria said, "I want to know and to see." She peered through the window and was startled to see the convoy of Nazi soldiers. She ran to her room and got dressed. Quietly she walked behind Michal. He opened the outside door very slightly. He was afraid when he heard that the Nazi may take him to the Army. He was afraid to go outside.

"Tata, I can go out. I am not afraid them," Maria said as she stepped outside the door and slowly walked towards the porch. To make sure she was safe, she looked back at her father to see if he was watching her.

As Maria walked further towards the center of the courtyard, she did not see the Nazi officer on horseback galloping towards the house. Suddenly, the man on horseback pulled up the reins and stopped, just in front of Maria. She was startled. Maria looked up at him, afraid that his horse would jump on her. When the officer pulled up the reins once again, the horse rose high on his both of his front, but quickly settled down as the officer released the reins. Maria never saw a tall, uniformed man sitting so upright on a beautiful horse that listened to each command the officer gave it. Maria was used to her farm horses, although friendly to her, were not for riding. Although Michal sometimes rode them for a short ride on Sundays, they were used mostly for farm and forest work. At that moment, Maria froze. She stood like a statue, staring at the soldier. Even her eyebrows were frozen because she was so frightened. She could not look directly at him. The soldier cinched up the horse, and moved his riding crop in front of the horse's mouth. As the horse slowed down and got closer to Maria, the officer pulled up on the reins and stopped the horse in front of Maria. He sat firmly in the saddle, with his handgun attached to his belt.

Michal looked behind the door that was ajar and softy called, "Maria, come back. Come back to house."

However, Maria could not hear him. "Come, come," the officer said as he raised his hand and beckoned with his finger for Maria to come to him. Maria could not move. The officer did not give up and called her again, "Come here, come here." Michal watched, sweating and holding his breath. Maria slowly relaxed as she saw that the horse was calming down and moving his head down. The officer smiled. She walked slowly towards the horse as the officer moved his right hand and put it inside his jacket. Michal almost threw opened the door, ready to run to Maria because he was afraid that the officer was going to hurt Maria. But just at that moment, the officer quickly pulled out a small wrapped package and gave it Maria. Michal saw that Maria was safe, so he stayed where he was. He watched Maria while she looked at the package. "What is it?" she asked the officer.

The officer smiled at her and said in German, "Open," while he gestured with both hands to open the package.

Maria carefully looked at the small package wrapped in brown paper, not sure what she should do. Then she looked back at the door and saw her father, hidden partially by the door, nodding his permission to open the package. Maria opened the package and was surprised to see it was chocolate. "Thank you, thank you," she told the officer, and ran back to the house. The officer, smiling, turned his horse towards the road and left. Michal happily opened the door for Maria. It was then he noticed that two soldiers were walking out of the barn, with one of his horses.

Michal ran towards the stable, forgetting the danger, and loudly pleaded, "Please do not take my horse, please do not take my horse," but the soldiers pushed him aside. They pointed to the barn trying to communicate that they were going to leave one horse behind. The soldiers were everywhere. The entire encampment was covered with the straw taken from Michal's barn. He watched the soldiers collect their arms, regroup, and march towards the road. Motorcycles passed them as they crossed the courtyard and walked to the east of the village.

Michal walked back to the barn. He saw many soldiers by the river pulling a large wooden wheel wrapped with cable. They yelled, one over the other, "Move, move," and placed the cable near the riverbank between the trees. The other soldiers carried large, two-meter posts. They dug half-meter holes into ground, and placed them every fifty meters alongside the cable. Then they nailed metal warning signs on each post.

When they left, Michal went to the river and checked the cable. It was a quarter inch diameter cable. Then he read the writing in Polish, "Alert, stay away from the line of the cable. Removing or destroying of the cable is subject to military punishment." From the fear that his cows often graze the grass near the river and may step over and break it, he moved the cable inside the bushes.

Before he returned home, he walked over to the straw in the field in the hopes that some straw could be salvaged. He picked up some straw from the ground and then dropped it. The straw was useless now. Well at least they left my family alone, Michal thought, as he looked towards the mountains and headed home.

On September 4, 1939, the Nazis announced that the boundary of the Third Reich has been expanded, and that the entire region in lower Beskidy Mountains belonged to them. At the beginning of the occupation, the Nazi Army was welcomed with open arms by the German settlers. The settlers decorated their homes with Nazi flags and tossed flowers to the soldiers.

After they established their control of the region, they called for the residents to return to their homes, guaranteeing their safety. They posted at each major building and crossroad that the Nazis had been in the region for over 2,000 years, and that they only spoke Polish. They told all the residents to stay in the region, and to return to the Nazi police all firearms, explosive devices, radios, and bikes. The banks and Polish currency were changed to German marks. They abolished all social organizations and arrested their leaders identified prior to the war. With the new Nazi administration, they renamed all formerly Polish named streets to German streets. Only the German language was permitted in all administrative offices. The occupants worked hard campaigning to the Poles that they were all of German descent.

In order to be successful, the Nazis closed schools and tried to convince the students to become German citizens. That was not successful. They issued each non-German identification card "Kenkarte" to each resident of the region including Jewish families who also populated the region. Some of them spoke fluent German and had business ties with Germans. The new administration created an atmosphere of hate between the Jewish Poles and Nazis. Shortly after they enforced the edict that all Jews must wear yellow armbands, they enacted laws prohibiting Jews from changing their residence, and restricting travel outside of the region where they lived.

In early April 1943, all Jews in occupied Poland received notice that they were going to be resettled into ghettos and labor camps. However, some Jewish family who lived in the small community in Beskidy region and had good relations with minority Germans, counted on being treated differently, that the minorities will protect them, and so they decided to stay in the community, without realizing that the Jews who lived in Germany were expelled from their businesses and their homes. The Jewish were not aware that since 1940, the Nazi SS authorities established the largest of Nazi concentration death camp in Auschwitz, where Jewish, Polish and other ethnics group perceived the enemies of Nazi state were exterminated in gas chambers, and used as slave labor. The SS, with the network of spies, had a list of names and locations for all Jewish families and Jewish business owners, from the small grocery store owner on up. The Nazis enforced the order to expel all Jews from their homes and businesses across the Beskidy region. The SS special unit without any mercy carried the Nazis' order, and by end of the April the SS armed with machine guns and police dogs, entered a Jewish owned small grocery store located near the center of the Milowka. "What is your name?" they shouted at the store clerk who was wearing a long beard.

"Jan is my name," the clerk replied, "and no I am not Juden. I work here. I like to work here," he went on, nervously shaking. "I do not own the store. Jakob owns the store and he is in his house."

"Over there," he said and pointed towards the house attached to the store, its overhead roof seen through the glassy iron door.

The SS man pushed him to the end of the counter. "Stay here and do not move," he ordered as he waved his shotgun in front of him.

Jan with his frightened face could not speak any words, only obeying the SS commands. "Fred," one SS called across the room to the other guard with his leashed dog. The guard dog sniffed the floor and quickly pulled the guards behind the counter towards Jan, and again sniffed Jan's apron soaked with smoked meat. He feared the dog, afraid that he was going to attack him. The SS men pulled the dog back to him. Then he shook his finger towards him, the dog obeyed and sat in front of him. Jackob overheard the voices of the Nazis entering into the hallway, and he hurried back to his room. It was too late as he heard again, "Halt, halt!"

Then the SS confronted him and he lifted his hand, pointed towards Jackob and saluted, Heil Hitler," but Jackob did not respond. The SS man pushed Jackob against the wall.

The SS asked Jakob his name and if he was the owner. "Yes," Jakob said.

They pushed Jakob against the wall, using their guns as sticks. They told him, "Call out for your family and tell them to come to the store now."

Jakob's ten-year-old son Feliks heard the SS, and quickly ran to hide under the wooden steps in the storage area behind the hallway. Through the slats, he saw the SS push his father against the wall. "Luba, come here," Jakob yelled to his daughter. "Sonia, come here," Jakob called to his wife. However, Jakob did not call for Feliks.

The other SS soldiers entered the living room. Luba and Sonia were sitting on the small couch. "Get up, get up!" the SS shouted as they shoved Luba and Sonia towards the door. "Where is the rest of your family? We know you have a boy. He is on our list. Where is Feliks?" the SS grilled Jakob again.

"I do not know where he is," Jakob said. Standing closer to Jakob, the SS pushed his gun into Jakob, smashing his face against the wall. Still, Jakob did not tell the SS where Feliks was.

Two SS came with their dogs; they searched the house and the store upside down, then stopping at the steps where Feliks was hiding. In the dark corner, Feliks was hiding, curled up in a tight ball. "Come here," the SS ordered Feliks, but Feliks did not move. The SS called again "Come here." Still Feliks did not move. The police dogs were barking frantically trying to get at Feliks. That only caused Feliks to retreat further.

Jakob was afraid that the dogs would attack his son, so he called out to Feliks, "Come over here, my son." Feliks, hearing his father call to him, crawled out from under the stairs.

The moment he emerged from the stairs, the SS grabbed him by his hands and pulled him towards the doorway. "You filthy liar, Jew!" he screamed.

Jan, the clerk in the store, was frightened. He stood by the counter and watched helplessly as Jakob with his family were escorted outside the store. Jakob looked at Jan and said, "Please take care of my business. I will return."

"What did he say?" the SS asked the Polish speaking SS. Then he chuckled as he heard the interpretation. The truck slowly approached the sidewalk in front of Jakob's bakery. "Get in, get in!" the SS screamed at the family as they pushed them inside the truck. Several other families were already inside and looked up silently at Jakob and his family. The truck proceeded along the village road escorted by Nazi soldiers on motorcycles. As the truck entered the small plaza, there were hundreds of villagers corralled in the center, surrounded by SS soldiers. They all stopped. Over loudspeakers, the SS announced that anyone who helped hide the Jews would be sent to labor camps.

At the corner, there were more Jewish families waiting as the SS forced other Jews towards the trucks. Some of the old people had a hard time trying to hoist themselves into the trucks. The SS pushed them along, prodding them with their guns. "Move, move!" the SS continued to yell as others already inside the truck helped the new arrivals into the trucks. The three trucks were packed. The SS closed the doors in the back, and locked them with pins. Mothers held their small crying children close in an effort to comfort them. Old men and women comforted each other as best they could. Older children were talking loudly so that the guards could not hear the younger children's cries. "Shut up!" the guard yelled while waving his gun. However, no one listened. The guard yelled louder, "Shut up, shut up!" When he threatened to shoot, everyone stopped talking except one child who continued to cry. An old man gave the mother a blanket. She wrapped the child in a blanket trying to keep him quiet. Pulling the child against her chest, she bent her head towards the child, her tears spilling over, mingling with those of her sobbing child.

From inside the truck, Jakob found small cracks in the canvas. He could peep through the cracks. He saw pine and oak trees near the road and saw that they were passing through several villages. Eventually the driver slowed down. They were entering a narrow road inside a city. Then they stopped at the town center. There Jakob saw many vendors selling vegetables, and crowds of people buying and selling. Alongside the road there were Nazi soldiers marching and saluting. SS on motorcycles were escorting trucks containing Jews from other small towns and villages.

At the plaza there were many civilians shopping. A few of the older Jews called on Jakob and got closer to him as the truck slowed down. They asked him, "Why only us are going to the labor camp?"

But Jakob, for the moment, was silent. He didn't have the answer. He said to the old man, "I do not understand why they were not with us, why we were separated from others. Are we special people?"

"Look, look," the old man said again as he pointed at the old courthouse walls draped with a large Nazi flag with black cross. Jakob saw Nazi flags displayed on all the houses as well. This was not the town as Jakob remembered.

"Father, why are we not stopping? This is Zywiec town, a county capital. Where are we going? You told me that we were going to town."

Jakob answered, "Yes, son, we are going little farther to another town. Do not worry, my son. We are going to see a new place and it is not that far away from our home. The Nazis told us that we are going to work at the labor camp and we will return after we finish our work."

"But Father," Stas said, "you told me that we always have a lot of work in our store. Why did they take us? Why are so many people going with us?"

He could not stop asking questions about the unknown destiny of the trip. He was only twelve years old. What could he understand? Jakob only wanted to be his father. Jakob tried to prepare his son for whatever the future might bring, but he had no answers himself. To make him comfortable Jakob asked, "Son, do you remember the words to this song?" as he hummed the melody.

"I know the song," his son said. "So, sing with me," Jakob said.

They were humming then softly began singing the words until the others heard and started to sing aloud. The angry driver pounded on the window trying to stop the singing, but the song carried them on. They drove across the farmland, alongside the railroad tracks. Trains passed by, whistling to announce the upcoming column of SS traffic which needed to cross the railroad tracks. The column of upcoming trucks yielded and stopped. All the truck's passengers were behind several units of soldiers riding on trucks. All of them stopped to sing. Jakob looked to the rear and saw the train station. The road was closed until the train passed, leaving the sound of the whistle behind. As the train rounded the curve, Jakob briefly saw cattle wagons crowded with people. No one waved at them. A few minutes later, the ramps opened, and the convoy of trucks entered inside the station along with a long line of train cars. The truck drivers followed towards the yellow building and small railroad station. The drivers parked behind other trucks already crowded with prisoners. The soldiers opened the trucks and led the passengers to the cattle cars, packing them in as many as 100 in a car. Jakob pulled his wife and two children into the corner and sat on his small suitcase. "Come sit on my lap," he said to the children and his wife. They gathered close and leaned into the corner. The passengers were exhausted from the trip. None of them had more than a few swallows of water and a bit of food. No one knew where their destination. Other passengers asked Jakob if he knew where they were. "Near Zywiec town," he said. As the travelers settled inside the cars, Nazi guards sealed them in. There was no chance to open the car from the inside. The cars' windows were small rectangles allowing no chance of escape. The train waited and waited. Many travelers were weak and fell to the floor. Eventually the train moved and slowly passed through town. Then it sped up, passing villages and small towns.

At four in the evening, the train arrived at Auschwitz. Slowly it passed through the gate and stopped near the long concrete platform. The doors were opened. Jakob called to his wife to wake up. "Where are we?" she asked.

Jakob said, "I think we're at the labor camp."

Strange men, some of them in striped pajamas, greeted Jakob and his family. They saw the SS wearing hats with skulls standing in front of the train in intervals of ten meters. The officer in charge stood with his Alsatian dog and watched all. Jakob could hear yelling, "Out, out, everyone! Leave your belongings in the train." Jakob held his family close, trying desperately to reassure them that all would be fine. Jakob's wife and children were too frightened to cry. The SS shouted out, "Men this way, women that way." Although the families tried to hold on to their children, the SS separated them, using their clubs to beat them apart. Jakob did not want to let his wife go. Although he tried to hold on to his wife and daughter, the SS struck both of his hands with a club.

Jakob wanted to hit him back, but the other SS with the dogs often were agitated, and poised to bite. Jakob cried out, "My children my children, my wife my wife," as an SS man hit him with the butt of a rifle. Jakob's wife and children were quickly pushed to the other side.

As they were swept along, Jakob's wife and children looked behind, but they could no longer see Jakob. "Tata, Tata!" they cried out, but there was no chance to say goodbye. Each traveler become a prisoner who was frightened by the barking SS dogs.

"They are just children, please, please do not harm them," Jakob begged the SS. His pleading went unanswered as he saw his wife and children sent to the other line.

Jakob and others turned their heads to look for one last moment as they were pushed by clubs to stay straight. "Why were these children taken from their parents?" Jakob said to another prisoner who was a Gypsy. "They just started their lives. What crime did they commit?"

From Jakob's line, the SS doctor walked alongside and quickly inspected the old and sick, separating them from the young and strong men. An old man close to Jakob looked up with frightened eyes. He laid his hands over Jakob, and with a final quick prayer said, "Be strong, be strong. You must survive. You must survive to tell the world." Before he was able to finish, the SS pushed him aside. Jakob acknowledged his understanding by moving his head down, and promising him as he looked deep into the old man's eyes.

The selections were quick and efficient. Only the strong remained. The prisoners were ordered to march in two rows to a gray concrete one-story building. As Jakob walked towards the building, one guard said to him, "You are filthy dirty. You must go and take a shower." At the shower room, the ice cold water coming from the pipes burst over the prisoners causing them to scream out loud. Jakob held his breath as the water hit his head. They only had a few minutes to go through the line and step outside the shower room into another room where prisoners were distributing prison uniforms. Everyone received ragged, ill-fitting striped uniforms and wooden shoes.

After the shower, Jakob and other prisoners were ordered to march to one building where two guards directed them to a long line. Jakob was next. "You, pull up the sleeve of your shirt." Then the nurse told him to place his left arm on the table. He saw the surgical tools and turned his head away. He felt the needle as he was tattooed with a number. Jakob clenched his teeth and held his breath. It was fast. The number was in blue. Now he thought, I am no longer a person. As he leaned forward to say this out loud to another prisoner, a guard struck him with a gun yelling, "No talking!"

"Next please," the SS called to the other prisoner standing in the line behind. Jakob, the gypsy, and a Polish young man followed the steps behind the columns of men.

"Why are we here?" Jakob asked the young men the SS caught me as polish priest, and resistance to Nazi, we are not allowed to talk as he whispered to Jackob. They followed the guard to the other building where prisoners worked as barbers. The barbers efficiently and quickly shaved the prisoners' heads.

After his head has been shaved, Jakob was ordered to go to block 21. The barracks had ten-foot walls and the roof rose another 15 feet to a peak of 22 feet. The entire barracks was divided by partition into two parts. On both sides of the walls there were three levels of narrow cells, where three people lived in each cell. The barracks had very little room to accommodate new arrivals.

The guards to a specific area directed Jakob and other prisoners. "You go here," the guard said to Jakob. It was at the end of the barracks as he found three tiers. "Here is your place," the capo said.

The prisoners welcomed him from their bunks, laying down and watching others as they looked for their beds. Jakob was thirsty. He saw near the door a bucket of water thick with insects. He quickly put his hand inside the bucket, shook the insects from his hands, and drank the water.

As he reached his bunk, he introduced himself. Two responded, "I'm Karol, my name is Herik." Jakob asked them if the water in the bucket was all they had to drink.

Karol and Herik replied, "Yes. To get good water, we are praying for rain." Jakob went to his place, climbed over the third tiers with two very skinny prisoners, and found his mattress - a burlap sack filled with straw. He sat at the edge of the bunk and laid his face against the railing. He held his eyes closed, recalling his wife and children left behind.

At dawn the next morning the capo threw open the barrack doors and called for roll call. The capos turned loudly barking dogs loose in the barracks. Jakob did not know what was happening as he watched the other prisoners run towards the front of the barrack with cups and spoons in hand. Jakob asked Karol what he should do. "We must form a group of five, stay with me," Karol said. As they finished forming the line, the SS trooper came and counted, one, two, three, four, five. After the count, he looked at the list and ordered that each new prisoner be given a metal cup and spoon. Breakfast, such as it was, was served.

Jakob saw the portion of breakfast he would receive: two slices of bread with little margarine and a taste of marmalade, and coffee. "Is that all we get for breakfast?" Jakob asked the other prisoner near him.

"Yes," the other prisoner said.

Jakob tested the coffee and spit it out. "What a terrible taste," he said.

"Do not do that," the other prisoner warned, whispering to Jakob because the capos were standing nearby. He said, "You must get used to it. You're lucky that they did not see you spitting. Last week, one prisoner spit his coffee, they took him away, and I never saw him again."

After breakfast, the prisoners marched into the middle of the plaza divided by a barbed wire fence. They were forced to dig drainage ditches alongside the roads. The capos and SS supervised all the work. Near where the men were working there was a double row of electrified fence surrounding the camp. There were large signs warning of the electrified fence. At noon, the capo called for lunch which consisted of a potato, turnip, or cabbage soup. For supper, there was coffee and a piece of bread with a small slice of sausage, margarine, jam, or cheese. Jakob, as a baker, learned to use the calories from the bread crust, always waiting to eat the crust last. He slowly chewed the crust and swallowed as he felt his stomach cramp inside his empty belly.

Three months later at 5:00 a.m., there were two prisoners missing at the roll call. The prisoners had escaped overnight. As soon as the prisoners were discovered missing, the search began. Sirens went off. However, they could not be found inside or near the barracks. Dozens of SS and their dogs, aided by local police, looked for them outside the camp. Still, the prisoners could not be found. The SS were very angry and called the prisoners to another roll call. The SS officer, with his cold face and his hat up above his eyebrows, walked alongside the rows and with a long stick poked each prisoner counting one, two, three – up to ten. Jakob watched for a moment, and then closed his eyes. He was shivering from fear that he was next in line to go; he held his breath. As the SS officer counted off, each prisoner who was the tenth was led off to be marched to his death. The rest of the prisoners were ordered to go back to work at the ditches through the camp, and to lay sod alongside the banks of the ditch. The others were sent to work on construction and repairing the barracks and the potholes in the roads they filled with gravel and sand.

This was their daily work until the fall 1943 when the capos came to Jakob's barracks and selected prisoners who either looked sick or could no longer work. When Jakob saw that his fellow prisoner with whom he shared a bed was collapsing from weakness, falling on the ground, he reached his arm to keep him steady. However, the prisoner was too weak and collapsed. The capo struck Jakob with rifle butt telling him, "You take him to the dump truck" and watched Jakob as he carried him on his shoulders and slowly placed him over the top of the truck between other weak prisoners condemned for death. They were to be transported to the crematory. As Jakob walked away from the truck, the capo called at him, "You will go to another part of the camp." The capo counted up to 100 prisoners and then gave them a sign to follow Jakob.

The prisoners were marched between the SS and posts of barbed wire and near the machine gun manned guard towers. Jakob heard children yelling. They were near the block where the children were sweeping the plazas alongside the barracks. Jackob with other inmates stopped for a moment, and looked across the fenced blocks and saw many children at work. As they marched further inside the camp, Jakob overheard capos who spoke Polish and German. He looked at them and saw that a few of the capos were Jewish. Jakob and others in his group were hopeful that they would survive because the capos would be less cruel to fellow Jews. They went inside housing that was better than what they had left behind. It was less crowded, housing 300 to 400 men sleeping double or triple to a bed. In the evening, the capos called the prisoners for supper. Jakob got soup with two small potatoes and a thin slice of meat. Then he stirred the soup. It was just a thin, almost colorless liquid, barely offering any resistance to the spoon. The next morning, the capo came into the barracks, blowing his whistle. This time he was without the dogs. After they called the daily roll call, they counted each prisoner and gave them one piece of bread with margarine and a cup of coffee. Jakob learned from previous experience that the coffee was awful and was surprised to find it drinkable. He was also surprised to find that the bread was more edible than the bread he had previously received.

Shortly after breakfast they were forced to work. The Nazis assigned the capos to guard the prisoners. The capos also were in charge of the barracks. Each day Jakob was assigned to unload gravel and coal from trains. He did this until winter arrived.

It was early morning as the frosty snow blew through the camp. The prisoners reported to work at the train station. Jakob and the other prisoners were clothed only in undershirts and a thin striped coat. The temperature reached 10 below zero. As the prisoners turned their backs against the freezing wind to protect their faces, one capo turned to Jakob and his two friends saying, "You come over here. Unload the steel beams." As the others were unloading the first pile, one prisoner dropped the end of the slab. The skin on his hands skin sloughed off. There was blood dripping down. The capo called him over and took him away.

One inmate close to Jackob bent quickly and grabbed a pile of snow into his palms, and rubbed against, and said to Jakob, "Take the snow to your hands, do it as I do but fast."

Jackob grabbed a pile of snow and rubbed it quickly against his hands, he felt cold and froze. To avoid the capos, Jakob turned towards the pile of steel bars and rubbed his hands more. He looked on his fellow inmates, bent his head towards him as he felt his hands warm and started to lift the heavy piles of steel with help from the others. Although his hands were bright red, no skin was coming off. They continued to work until lunch. "Thank you," Jakob said to other inmates. "You saved my hands. I do not know how I can pay you back."

"Do not worry, my friend," the inmate said, "we all must stick together, we must survive."

Jakob told them of his experience with the old man at the platform.

"Yes, I promised him when we first arrived that I would do whatever I could to survive and help other prisoners if I can."

After ten hours of grueling work, several prisoners could not handle the cold and fell to the ground. The capo beat them and they took them away in the truck. Jakob and the rest of the prisoners returned to barracks. They were glad to at least keep warm. Each prisoner received his ration of approximately a quarter of inch thick slice of bread with black coffee. They all were hungry and tired, and quickly fell sleep.

As the spring arrived and the snow melted in the mountains, the river collected more water, washing away the pasture and meadows. Nazi settlers requested the Nazi authorities to make new channels and to construct dams to prevent further erosion of prime farmland. The Nazi authorities requested from headquarters that laborers be sent from Auschwitz to work on the dam project. In mid-spring, the first convoy of prisoners arrived to construct the dam. The Auschwitz authorities chose a hundred men from the Birkenau site of the camp to work outside of the labor camp.

For three months, Jakob observed that at the fifth barracks, somewhat away from his barracks, after early morning roll call the Nazi guards forced several groups of inmates to the trucks, and drove them out of the camp. Each evening they returned, and all inmates were exhausted, but some of them were so weak they could not walk back to the barracks. One night, Jakob, with the help of two other prisoners, quietly left their bunks and snuck out from the barracks. They were careful to avoid the lights from the guard towers. They eventually reached the fifth building where the prisoners who were working on the dam resided.

"What are you doing here?" one prisoner whispered to Jakob's group.

Jakob said, "I want to go tomorrow to work with this group." Jakob saw that the prisoners were returning each night, hungry, thirsty and exhausted. Some of them were so weak that they could not go back to the work site the following day. Jakob tried to find out why, but he could not get the answer. Most of the other prisoners with whom he wanted to talk to spoke languages other than Polish. When Jakob would ask them questions, they would only shake their heads, no, no.

Then one day at the roll call, a very small older Polish inmate who was an artist, who had worked in the past with Jewish businesses, overheard Jakob asking this same question. "Come here," he said. "Get closer to me, but watch out for the capos."

"Every morning, the SS take us to a village two-hours away from here. We are working at the river. It is hard work, but we can get better meals and fresh water. The SS guards force us to work in the very cold river."

He quickly became quiet as he saw a capo approach telling Jakob, "I cannot talk to you more. I will tell you more later."

Evening came and every inmate had to be counted in the barn. The armed guards were closely watching all the inmates. Jakob went to sleep hoping that he would be chosen the following day to work outside the camp. He dreamt about the routes as the other prisoners described, and his struggle to fight with the two guards. The dream made him a little more hopeful that one day he would win his freedom.

Every day at the roll call he showed the guards that he was strong and able to work. He had to hide. Each time he had to lift a heavy load of construction materials, he turned his head away from the kapos so that they could not see the grimace of pain on his face.

At the end of May, the SS, escorted by the capos, came to the camp to select healthy and strong inmates. They inspected the rest of the inmates in the other two barracks as well, and then called on capos to remove the sick and weak from the barracks, and deport them to the gas chamber. Because these inmates were unable to work, there was no purpose for them to stay alive. The SS officer walked alongside the rest of the inmates. In his hands he held a short leash. The officer chose ten or more inmates. Jakob was thinking, *pick me, pick me.* Then the SS officer softly tapped Jakob on his right shoulder telling him, "You, step out from the row." He looked at Jakob and pushed him towards the other selected inmates.

The capo escorted one hundred inmates towards the camp's main road as the SS officers directed them towards the idling trucks. Already inside the trucks, inmates from the other barracks waited to depart for work. The SS separated the inmates by numbers, and added their names to their list. "Hurry up, hurry up!" they yelled as each inmate climbed inside the truck, pushing the other inmates aside. The trucks left the camp, escorted by armed SS in front and in back of each truck. They passed through small towns, and made several stops to let Nazi battalions cross. As they parked near the work area, the SS guards held their machine guns pointed towards the rear exit of the trucks, making sure that no prisoner had the opportunity to escape.

Jakob was in truck number four, near the barbed wire fence dividing the empty field and forest line. A few feet away from the rear of the truck on higher ground a guard held a list and called each prisoner's name to come out from the truck. Each prisoner's hands were tied, which made it difficult to jump from the truck and keep balanced upright. Some of them fell to their knees and were kicked by the guards to quickly get up and move away from the truck. Jakob was pushed to the middle of the truck as the inmates quickly jumped out.

Jakob heard someone quietly calling his name. "Yes," he answered, without thinking that there may be another Jakob. He rushed forward, between some other inmates, grabbed what he could for balance, and jumped out of the truck. He managed to jump without falling. The guards separated them into two groups. Jakob's group consisting of about 20 inmates was ordered to march towards the storage shed near several large pine trees. Inside the shed were shovels and heavy hammers, which were hung on the walls. Jakob picked up a shovel walked quickly to his group, already in formation. The guards yelled to hurry up, and directed the inmates to march alongside the riverbank. Jakob kept his head straight, and like a soldier walked with his shovel holding it like a rifle, exactly as he had seen the Nazi soldiers do it.

Jakob saw the mountains, the forests, and the barbed wire, and he dreamed and planned his escape. A couple of hundred feet from the riverbank were rows of pine and other trees. On the other side of the bank was flat pasture land, bordering the village. Oftentimes the land was flooded. On the orders of Nazi settlers, the inmates constructed a new river channel with shallow ramps every one hundred meters. With the new river embankment, they placed large rocks to prevent further erosion.

The current varied in depth from steep to shallow. When looking at the river, Jakob's thoughts went far back to historical times. He heard the voice of Moses when he spoke "let my people go." But Jakob thought there are other inmates from other backgrounds. Let them all go. For a moment he closed his eyes and pictured the river disappearing about a half a mile away, behind a hill thick with bushes and pine trees. On both sides of the river, about one hundred feet apart, were tall watchtowers. Inside the towers were sandbags reaching the top of the walls. Two guards inside were armed with machine guns, which were pointed towards the riverbank and the inmates. There was also a double strand of barbed wire stretched between the towers.

Jakob's dream of escaping was just a dream. After he surveyed how detailed the Nazis were in mapping out the placement of the guard towers, he realized that there was little chance for escape. Jakob's fellow inmates could not talk. They knew their only hope of surviving was to be silent, and not to have dreams of freedom. Although the work along the riverbank was relentless and hard, the inmates were somewhat relieved that they had the opportunity to just breathe fresh air, drink fresh water, and be away from the death camp. "Halt!" one of the guards shouted to Jakob's group. Jakob's heart raced and his lips trembled. "What I have done," he said to himself.

Then he heard again, "Stop." One of the SS guards fired his rifle into the air.

All the inmates stopped to let the last prisoner join them at the end of the group, and then all were ordered to march. "Stop here," the guard ordered. They were near the riverbank. Jakob looked down from the riverbank as the rushing water reflected the morning sun. He placed his shovel in front of him as did the rest of inmates. "Here you will start to work," the guard said loudly as he took his gun from his holster and pointed it towards the inmates. The only solace the inmates could take was that at least they were out in the fresh air. The smell of the pine trees gave them some measure of comfort.

The first group of inmates entered the river, spacing themselves approximately ten feet apart. The guard pointed the gun at Jakob, telling him, "move, move." At that moment, Jakob slipped down the embankment and hit the icy water – hard. After the initial shock of the cold water, Jakob's mind flashed back on the first moment in Auschwitz when the inmates were forced to take showers in very cold water right after their arrival at the labor camp. He tried to shake the memory away, but he could not. Jakob's shovel flew over his head, landing in the rushing water. As he saw the strong current submerge the shovel, Jackob fear the imminent danger to lose his life. *What I will do now, the shovel is more important to the Nazis than my life. What punishment will I get, even the threat of death.* The guards were shouting at him, "Go get the shovel!" and laughed loudly. He ran after the shovel down the river and stumbled over the slippery rocks,bruised his leg, then saw fenced barbwire touching the water level across the river with two guards walking on each side of the riverbank, worried that he would never be able to get the shovel, he could not cross the side, and this will be certain death. The shovel was trapped over the fence. Jackob feared for his life, he quickly grabbed the shovel and rushed over the bank hoping that the guard would not do him harm.

Jakob knew he had only seconds to and get back to work. The guards were watching him, laughing sadistically. The guard dogs were straining at their leashes. Within moments, Jakob knew the guards would release the dogs on him and he would be eaten alive. He returned to the group of inmates. Some of the inmates already were working around the eroded bank trying to stabilize the slope. They pushed heavy wheelbarrows filled with rocks and dumped them over. They broke up the large rocks using hammers.

One of the inmates who was pushing the wheelbarrow lost his strength and fell to the ground. He pulled his knees towards his chest behind the wheelbarrow. The guard grabbed a bucket of water and threw it in the prisoner's face all the while yelling at him to stand up. When the inmate couldn't stand, the guard kicked him hard in his back. The prisoner rolled up in a ball in extreme pain. He tried to reach the handle of the wheelbarrow, but fell down. The guards pushed him aside. The guards ordered two other inmates to come over and pick up the other badly beaten prisoner. The two inmates dragged the half-dead man into the forest. Two guards went with them. Soon after, Jakob heard the sound of gunfire. He knew that the man had been executed.

After yet another grueling day, the whistle finally announced that the workday was over. Jakob's hands were blistered after having spent the day breaking up rocks with the heavy hammer. The inmates were ordered to form this same line as they had first thing in the morning. The guard checked the list, calling out each name. The guard called

Franek, but no one responded. Franek was the inmate who had been executed earlier in the day. When the guard finished calling out names, he directed the inmates to march back to the waiting trucks.

Jakob was exhausted, his entire body writhing in pain. No prisoner dared complain out loud for fear of immediate retribution. All anyone could do was hang his head and try to sleep for few moments as the truck bounced over the rough country road on the way back to the camp. It was dusk by the time the truck returned to camp. Upon arrival at the camp, Jakob noticed that new inmates had arrived. They were being checked by the gate guards and ordered to the barracks. Most of the inmates were already in their beds. The guards turned off the dim lights.

Jakob found his bunk, which was near the door. He laid down and could feel the warm marsh air coming in through the cracks in the wall. He covered his ears so as not to hear the noises from the other inmates, and quickly fell asleep.

Over the next two weeks, the early morning roll call was especially difficult on the inmates. The inmates knew that they had to respond to the roll call quickly or their punishment would be severe. Jakob slid from his upper bunk and lined up for roll call with the rest of the inmates. Jakob and the rest of the inmates were sore; not only from their wooden slat bunks that passed for beds, but also because of the physically grueling work they were forced to perform from sun up to sun down, seven days a week.

At the end of the second month, the Nazi camp director appointed a new commander to oversee the river project. He received from the director of the camp a long list of inmates to work outside of the camp. The inmates received their daily breakfast, a half-liter of unsweetened black coffee with tea with a slice of bread with margarine. They had to eat the little food quickly as the commander set the time and called on inmates to form two rows. He looked brutal as he walked among the inmates parading his power of life or death that he could execute with one stroke of his finger. He reviewed a long list of the inmates to ensure that no one had escaped from the unit of barracks overnight. Then he called on each inmate from the rows, and some were sent back to their barracks by pointing at them. As he continued to read, the loud siren broke from the watchtower in the next block and the commander immediately stopped to read, looked at the tower, and waited for guard's sign. The inmates whispered to each other, praying that no inmates had escaped. Jackob stood and kept his emotions inside and was very nervous. To help his emotions he twisted his fingers as he held his both hands behind his back. The commander swiftly turned and then walked behind the group in front and moved his baton in hurry and folded the list. Jakob worried why he has not finished reading the list, as he wanted to be included for the outside camp work. The Nazi commander rotated his baton and swung it around, and then pointed to inmates. He bypassed Jakob, but then he turned his head and looked back at him. With a stern face, the commander asked Jakob, "What is your name?"

Jackob said, with as much conviction as he could muster, "Jakob."

The commander did not ask anyone else their name, saying, "You will go with the group," as he moved his button against him. Then he continued walking alongside the line of standing inmates, and counted how many he had chosen for the river work. He pointed at the last counted inmates and separated the others in the line. He called on the other kapo, "Take them with you to work on the camp ditches on the other side to camp. Then return to choose inmates and force them to march towards the trucks standing near the watchtower."

There were no seats in the trucks, so all the men had to stand. At least, they thought, their hands were not shackled so they could use them to hold on. The truck was crowded. There was no room to move about. Jakob was near the rear exit. They were driving over a dirt road going uphill when some of the inmates lost their ability to hold onto the railing. They were pushed to the rear of the truck. Jakob held on. Several other inmates helped him hold on. Then the truck hit a deep pothole, which caused Jakob to bounce back towards the other inmates.

The thick fog still hung over most of the valley when the inmates arrived. With the light visibility over the river, Nazi guards watched each inmate carefully as they were ordered to form two rows. "Halt!" the kapo called on one inmate who switched his position to the other side of the row. The kapos were suspicious that the thick fog may encourage the inmates to run away from the worksite. The inmates waited until the fog settled down and the kapo called on inmates to work. Jackob with other inmates had the assignment near the pile of rocks stacked away from the riverbank. "You," the capo called on them, "you will cut the stones," he reiterated again to them. The rest of the inmates were ordered work at the river and at the riverbank.

At mid-morning, all inmates were exposed to the heatwaves as the sun rose above the center of the valley, and the humidity was so high that some inmates had become very weak. The inmates sweated as they loaded the wheelbarrow with crushed stones and carried them near the riverbank. Jackob had become weak and very thirsty, his mouth dried out and cracked, his lips, too, and he could feel scratches inside his mouth and throat. "I could jump to the river, and have some water," he said to his inmate friend. His temptation was very high, and he turned and saw guards armed with machine guns. When the guards marched to the other side, Jackob whispered to the other inmates, "Let us drop the stones over the water and push the wheelbarrow near the edge to drop the stones over." He stood near the bank's edge, the water splashed over them and reached their faces, giving them at least some relief.

By very early in the afternoon most of the inmates were so exhausted from the heat, they could barely do any work. The guards yelled, "Shnell, shnell!" and called at them with warning signs as they pointed their guns towards them. Shortly after they heard thunder from the side of the mountains and looked at the sparse dark clouds as they glued to each other and created large balls. Then they felt a strong gust of wind that swept towards the valley of the pine trees and bent them as they leaned back and forth one over the other, creating a huge black wall covering with sudden darkness the entire view from the riverside. The dark clouds opened long streams of light and were followed by peals of thunder which shook the valley followed by a lightning bolt that smashed against the large lonely oak tree at the center meadow near the work camp, cutting it in half as the branches fell into the ground leaving a huge scar seen far away from the river. Some of the inmates started climbing over the embankment but the guards opened fire and shouted at them to get back to work. From Upper Mountain the river collected a large volume of water from the streams and rapidly became one large enough to tear down small trees and overflow the fields and with great force approached to the inmates' work site. The inmates panicked when they heard the thunder and saw a huge bulk of the water coming rapidly toward them. When they ran for cover, the guards started picking them off. The rushing water hit the guard towers with such force that the towers were pushed over. By the time the river had its way, the guard tower was nothing more than scrap. Jakob saw the towers being swept away. He ran with the other inmates to the edge of the bank and dove into the rushing water. At the same time, and from higher ground, the other guards began shooting at them. Bullets were flying everywhere. One shot hit Jakob's leg as he submerged. The waves pulled him under.

The brown river water washed away his blood as the rocks were rolling under his legs. Jakob came up for air. He still heard the guns and saw several bodies floating down the river. Another wave of water hit him in the face, causing him to tumble in the water once again. Even though Jakob fought the current, the pain of his injuries and the current pulled him to the bottom. Just as he came to the surface, exhausted, he saw a log floating towards him. He grabbed on. As he did so, he saw the guards nearby, as well as hearing their attack dogs barking.

Jakob all of a sudden had hopes that he actually might escape. He quickly swam under the log so that his body would be hidden from the guards. The roiling water continued to push him down river. At the narrowest part Jakob was pushed into some branches and then catapulted forward. Around the bend was a waterfall. Jakob flew over the falls, letting go of the trunk as he hit the water below. Gasping for air, Jakob finally made it to the surface. The current finally pushed him to more shallow water, where he was able to grab a foothold and down the river. His lungs could no longer hold the air and he fought with the current; he emerged above water and caught the air as his feet touched the bottom of the river.

Very weak, Jakob pulled himself from the river and moved as fast as he could to find cover in the nearby tall grass. He heard sirens and the barking dogs, *they must be very close to me.* He ran faster until he reached the edge of the thick forest bushes and fell on his knees and with both hands grabbed the end of the pine branches laying over the ground near the trunk covered over by more branches, and then he fainted from the pain of his injuries.

After many hours, Jakob woke up, shook his head slowly, and for a moment, he could not remember where he was as the pain increased in his leg. *How did I get here?* He slowly moved his wounded leg as he still was lying down, oh, ouch, he fought with his pain, as he turned around for his more comfortable position, and he bounced against the trunk and large pine branches above him surrounded by the other thick bark of pine trees.

It took him a while to get conscious when he heard the crows, kra, kra, kra, as they felt his presence. *I am in the forest I must be safe.* He crawled away from the thick branches as they were touching his back.

He crawled from his hiding place. *I must look for help* Jakob repeated to himself. After walking for about a half an hour, he could barely go on. Just as Jakob was about to give up, he saw a house and barn in the distance. He also heard barking dogs and motorcycles. He could see that the SS was at the house. Jakob waited until the SS were gone, and then walked slowly towards the house. He saw a small teenage girl, waved to her, and then fell to the ground.

Maria ran to house yelling, "Tata, Tata, there is man behind the barn. I just saw a man, and he was waving to me."

"Where?" Michal asked. "I don't see him."

As Michal walked behind the barn he heard a faint cry. Michal knelt down and immediately saw the Star of David on Jakob's prison uniform. "For moment, from the dear and danger Michael mind frozed" then he said, "you are the prisoner who escaped. The SS were here. They are all looking for the escaped prisoner."

He lifted Jakob from the ground and carried him into the house as Maria followed them.

"Neska, he needs help. He is hurt. Get some bed sheet to make bandages."

Neska saw the Star of David and said to Michal, "We must report him to the SS. You just heard what they said to us. If they find him here, we'll either be deported or killed."

"No, we're not going to turn him in. He's in our home. Look at the cross. You always pray. But now, when a stranger needs you, you turn away. Do as I say, and do it now. Make some bandages for this man."

Michal did what he could to bandage Jakob's wounds. He poured vodka over Jakob's wounds. He winced in pain. Then he took some fresh clothes from his closet and dressed Jakob. When he was done, he held a cup of warm tea to Jakob's lips and helped him drink the soothing liquid. After a few sips of the tea, Michal carried Jakob over to a bed. Jakob, his eyes tearing, said to Michal, "You are risking your life to help me. I must leave your home. Please help me find somewhere else to hide."

Meanwhile, Neska was nervously pacing from one room to another. She kept on looking outside to see if the soldiers were coming back. After his wounds were treated, Jakob slowly stood up and dressed in Michal's clothes. Although the pants were big, he was able to keep them up using a rope as a belt. "Jakob, this shirt will be good for you when you're in the mountains. It's still cold there, and you'll need a heavier shirt."

"Jakob, eat something. Neska made a soup." Jakob slowly touched the spoon and for a moment he just stirred the thick creamy soup.

"What, you don't like my soup?" Neska asked. Then he brought a spoonful to his mouth. The potatoes, carrots and chicken – food he had not tasted in months – was almost more than he could bear.

"No, no. The soup is very tasty. I have not eaten such good food for a long time."

After supper, Michal took Jakob to the storage room so that Jakob could get a good night's sleep. "Tomorrow we will travel to the mountains where you will be safe."

Early the next morning, as Neska and Maria were washing clothes in the river, they heard motorcycles approaching. Dropping the clothes, Neska ran to the house shouting, "Michal, Michal, the soldiers are coming!" Jakob heard her cries and jumped up from the bed. Panicking, Neska yelled at Michal, "Where are you going hide him? We will all die. We all be in Auschwitz. Take him out of here."

Michal was trying to think of a way to get Jakob to safety and at the same time not endanger his own family. He got some cow dung from his barn and dumped it on Jakob's boots. "Why are you doing this?" Jakob asked.

"Because the dung will disguise your smell to the dogs," Michal said. The smell made Jakob gag. "You'll be safe in the barn for the meantime. Eventually, the smell will go away," Michal told Jakob.

They could hear the sounds of motorcycles in the distance. "We have to hurry," Michal growled. Jakob ran to the barn and threw himself into the bale of straw until he reached bottom. The dust was suffocating. The motorcycles were close. Gathering his composure and taking a deep breath, Michal picked up the pitchfork and casually strolled around to the front of the barn, ready to greet the soldiers.

Everyone held their breath as the soldiers and their dogs searched the barn. Michal could hear his heart pounding in his chest. It took every effort to appear unconcerned to the soldiers. One of the soldiers stepped within inches of Michal's face. "You must immediately report to us if you see a prisoner or any partisan. It is forbidden for any person to assist the partisans or inmates. If we find out you or any member of your family did so, you will meet the same fate as the inmates."

As soon as the soldiers were out of sight, Michal went to check on Jakob. He told Jakob to stay put for another half an hour just in case the soldiers were planning on returning. Michal began to gather some food for Jakob to take with him later in the day. "Yes, Yes," Michal said, "I just prepared for him to leave to the mountains."

Neska crept behind Michal asking, "Is the Jew still here? If he is, get him out of here now. You're selfish to risk the lives of me and our children for just a Jew."

"You listen to me, Neska. Jew or not Jew, he is not a different then me, I will do whatever I can to help the man to survive the evil time, he suffer enough, Go get him a fresh set of clothes."

Taken aback by Michal's tone, she got the clothes and brought them to Jakob. "Let's go now," Turning to Maria, Michal told her to go outside and check to see if the road was clear. In the meantime, Michal hitched up the horse to the wagon. "Get in the wagon and cover yourself with straw," Michal told Jakob. Michal flicked the whip, and the horse took off running towards the forest. "Keep quiet," Michal whispered to Jakob. "Soon we'll be safe."

The road was full of holes, and Jakob was thrown every which way as the wagon crashed back and forth. Still, Jakob managed to hold on. "Michal, where we are going?" Jackob asked again.

"Do not worry," Michal said, "I will take you to small shelter, a cave deep in the thick forest, it is very safe and a good place to hide. It is better than to keep you in my basement or hide you inside the barn.

Now please be quiet," Michal again whispered and dropped more straw over Jackob and swung his reins over the horse and made him run over the farm field road. As they reached the forest edge and entered the narrow steep road, Michal stopped the horse. "Jackob, now you are safe, we are safe, you can sit t up, soon we must climb to the hills."

As the narrowed road ended and Michal dislodged his horse and dropped over his shoulders Jackob's supplies, he pulled him over a very narrow path covered by moss between trees. Jackob took from the wagon a small cane and leapt behind the horse path. When the path was too narrow for the horse to pass through, Michal tied the horse against a few pine branches and took the supplies from the horse and dropped them over his back. "Jackob, come with me, we must now cross the creek."

As they walked, Jackob's leg started to swell but he kept going, and in a few more minutes Michal called on Jackob. Then Michal slowly placed the bag of potatoes over the pine tree's branches and said, "Look behind the branches inside the rocks covered by bushes. This is your hiding place."

"Michal, I could never find the place."

"That's why I brought you here. You should be safe here. In addition, the trees will protect you from harsh winter and cold. Jackob, come here and look at the cave, but be careful not to trip over the stones."

Michal led Jackob towards the small opening as Jackob was blinded. "Where am I?" He turned his head, and behind him he saw a only small fragment of daylight. When Michal lit a candle, Jackob looked at the rocky walls around him, and said, "The cave is larger than I thought, it is good shelter for me. The cave can accommodate two or three people," Jackob said to Michal.

"Jackob, I will bring the rest of your supplies, you go out and cut some of the pine branches and carry them inside. We must construct a bed for you."

Michal returned from the horse and carried to the cave another bag of grain and large bulk of salt. "Now, Jackob, you can build fire only at night inside the cave near the exit, the smoke no one will see, but do not build the fire when the moon is full. Oh, I almost forgot," he added as he pulled out of his jacket several packages of matches, and gave them to Jackob.

"Remember," Michal said. "In the peak of the mountain, the SS have an observation camp, and they patrol the region so do not go far away from the cave. Next week I will come with my daughter Maria. I will show her how she can find you. She'll bring you food and basic supplies."

The first night in the cave, Jakob slept nestled under the hay. He couldn't help but dream about his life in Auschwitz. He relived the moments when he thought of escape by throwing his shirt over the electrified barbed wire fence and climbing over it. In his dreams, that plan never worked. He always ended up being electrocuted while the other inmates stood by and watched. Every time Jakob had this recurring nightmare, he would wake up in a cold sweat.

The search for escapees increased the presence of SS all over the village. They hunted their inmates as if they were animals using dogs and local spies. All villagers were afraid that some inmates would be hiding in the barns or in their properties. They were afraid of the terror from the SS. Michal's farm was no exception as they came late one afternoon onto Michal's property and quickly walked to the house and pounded the door. Stas with Anka ran to the other room and hid behind the bed. With fear of her own life, Neska called on Maria, "Go and open the door."

Maria hesitated, saying, "I do not want to go."

"You must go and open the door," Neska insisted.

Maria with the worst fear ever walked out from the leaving room, shot behind the door and reached the front house door and fearfully opened it, expecting the worst. "Heil Hitler," Maria said.

"Heil Hitler."

The SS guard looked her, stepped inside the house, then yelled at her and walked behind her to the kitchen door. Maria tried to conceal her fear by moving about the kitchen area, pretending to tend to the fire fueling the stove. "What are you doing?" the guard shouted at Maria.

"This is our supper and I just wanted to add more wood to keep it cooking," Maria said.

The SS asked Neska, "Where is your husband?"

Neska said, "He is working in the forest and should be here shortly."

"We will wait for him here," the SS officer said. "But he had better not have anything to do with the escaped inmates."

Neska told the officer, "I have never seen any inmates around this house. If I had, I would report them to you immediately."

The SS standing guard at the front of the house was the first to see Michal. He ran inside and, with the other SS men. As soon as Michal stepped through the door, the SS came out of their hiding places. "Where is the Jew? We heard that you saw him."

Glancing furtively at Maria in an effort to keep her quiet, Michal said, "I just came from work. I only brought the pine wood already dried ready to be used for the fire. You can check if you want."

"Where is the Jew?" again they asked, this time pushing Michal to the floor.

"I do not know what you are talking about. I have not seen any strangers in the village. I just work in the forest," Michal said.

The guard pushed him towards the door. "We will return, but if you will not report that you have seen the escapee, you all will be deported to Auschwitz." As abruptly as they entered the house, they just left. After they left, Michal and his family let out a collective sigh of relief. For a while, at least, the danger was gone.

By the end of the second week of Jackob's departure to his hiding place, someone in the village got very sick, and died from TB, and the German health authorities alarmed the police reporting that all villagers should be checked by the regional doctor in Zywiec town. The Nazis posted notice in the village that all farmers must be ready and be prepared to go to the clinic in Zywiec. Several large trucks with speaker announcements drove across the villages and pick up all families from their homes. On the way up to the village they stopped up the road over at Michal's farm. They forced all Michal's family into the truck with several other families already sitting inside. Once inside the truck, Michal and his family learned that one family who lived down the next village had serious TB symptoms and died.

Once inside the hospital court, the farmers' families worried and, scared, start to pray as they entered the hospital door. The police ordered that all families must stay together and they must undress. Each family member thoroughly was checked by the nurse, and then by the doctor. As it turned out, Michal and his family were free of TB. Michal knew that being diagnosed with TB meant instant deportation to the death camps. Michal sadly noticed that several families did not make the return trip to their villages.

It had been several weeks since Michal had visited Jakob hiding in his cave. This time Maria went with him. "Help me collect food to take to the cave," he told Maria. Michal and Maria left for the cave after the SS had already completed their patrol of his property. It was late morning, and Michal was glad to be in the forest where the trees sheltered him.

Jakob was adjusting well to his confinement in the cave. For the first time since the labor camp he felt strong and well. As he was preparing to eat some blueberries, he heard the branches crackle outside the cave. He stepped out and quietly approached the mouth of the cave and saw Michal with Maria approach from behind some nearby trees. Happily Jakob hugged both of them. "It's so good to see you," he said. "Michal, I was worried so much what happened to you. I thought the SS took you away and I would not see you again."

After Michal and Maria rested for a moment after their climb up the mountain, Michal started to tell Jakob what the SS had been up to. "They were in my house the day after I left you here at the cave. They waited for me, and they were looking for you and other escapees. They turned the house and barn upside down threatened to burn down my place."

"Do you know how many inmates survived?" Jakob asked Michal.

"I do not know," Michal said.

"They caught some inmates down by the village. They executed some of them in the plaza. All the villagers were required to witness the executions. It was very painful to see." Michal did not continue his story.

"I brought you two extra rabbit traps, but you may see a fox trapped. You must be careful to stretch the string very tightly so that when the trap springs, the force will kill the rabbit. Make sure that you do not put your hands inside the trap when setting it. You must be especially careful not to place the traps in open spaces where the Nazis will find them. If they find a trap, they'll know that someone is here and won't give up until they find you. The SS has not given up their search for you or other inmates. Each day they are searching the villages and small towns for remaining inmates. They have posted pictures of escaped inmates and have offered rewards.

"Jakob, I will not be able to visit you very often, but Maria will visit you and she will bring you more supplies from time to time. There are informants who aid partisans and the escaped inmates. No one knows who they are. There is great danger. Now we must go to the village," Michal said.

"Thank you," Jakob said as he hugged Maria one more time and shook Michal's hand. "I think I will survive."

With the fall arriving, near the cave the forest green sprouts of bushes attached to the creek edges and sparsely growing in small spots exposed to the sunny sky, steadily changed to fall color. In preparation for winter months Jackob collected from bushes dried blueberries and cranberries for his tea. For the next several weeks he collected mushrooms and dried them near the fire inside the cave. All his fall harvest was a supplement for his bag of potatoes and bag of grain. He felt more secure that he will have enough food to survive the harsh winter to come.

It was now over three months since Jakob started living in the cave. One day was like the next one. Jakob would inspect the perimeter of his cave to make sure that it was not visible from the outside. He would then check the animal traps. Although his leg was still hurting, he welcomed the brief exercise. Each day Jakob could hear distant gunfire. Oftentimes he heard planes overhead. As time went on, he no longer gave much thought to the SS patrols or local hunters.

At the end of the October 1943, the resistance against Nazi occupation escalated. The partisans regrouped in each part of the Beskidy region and the Nazis enforced strong laws against residents who aided the Nazi resistance. Michal with his five colleagues as usual worked days at the forest cutting selectively trees and hauling them to the wood mill at the town. Just before entering to the main road, Michal called on their colleagues. "We are trapped, the SS is in front of us. Gestapo blockaded the road." Michal again yelled, "What we should do?"

"Wait on the other side and walk towards the SS officer."

With anger the SS man said, "You aided the partisans and they killed two of our soldiers. Raise your hands." The other SS quickly surrounded the men. "You," one SS pointed his weapon at Michal, "take the horse reins," as they escorted them to the mill.

At the mill, the Nazi supervisor took Michal's horse's reins and drove the car towards the stored pile of wood. "You all must report to SS headquarters," the Nazi capo said. "You will go fight against the Russians on the Eastern Front."

Michal kneeled on the ground and raised his hands. "My family, I must see my family, and please let me go." All his pleading and begging were ignored, and then Michal saw more men in several groups near the mill guardhouse.

Shortly after the Michal arrest and other men in his group, a woman from the village, ran to Michal's farm. As she approached the house, Maria was hanging her wash on the porch. Ready to return to the house a woman approached. "Hello," the woman called to Maria and walked towards her. "Where is your mother?"

"She is not my mother," she said. "She is my stepmother."

"So where is she?" the woman asked again.

"She is in the house."

"Can you take me to her?"

Maria took her across the porch and Neska welcomed the woman. "I brought you very sad news. The Nazis arrested your husband with five other men. They may not come home; I think they took them to the Nazi Army."

"What?" Neska, disturbed and disbelieving, nervously shook. "To the Nazi Army? My husband, oh no, this cannot be true," Neska nervously repeated.

When Maria overheard, she ran from the house, fell over the porch, and cried, "My dear father, what happened to my father," as she could not stop crying. "What can I do without my father? My mother is not here and now my father is gone." She choked herself from her crying as the women walked outside the house. She grabbed Maria's hand. "My child, your father will return; do not worry, he will be back soon."

"No, no, I do not believe you!" She ran inside stable, and sought comfort with her little cow that she always loved.

The day after she received the terrible news that Michal was taken by the German Army, Neska immediately changed her behavior toward Stas and Hanka. She treated them badly each time they asked for more food or wanted to make a fire in their favorite wood stove. Neska sent them to their room. Maria could no longer take a loaf bread and butter and the lunch with chicken meat was rarely available for her. Each time when Neska cooked lunch, Maria had to help her, when the cooking was done; Neska portioned the lunch to Maria and Stas with Anka giving herself the most. It was little food, they were still hungry, and Maria asked Neska. "Mother, can I have more soup and meat?"

"I do not have more meat," she said as she held a big chunk of chicken meat in her hand as Stas and Hanka watched. Shortly after lunch, Hanka and Stas walked into their room but Neska called on them. "Go with Maria and help her to clean the stable." Neska said to Maria, "Take them with you," as she placed the butter and bread inside the cabinet and locked it. She held the key in her hand until Maria left the room.

It was several weeks later; Maria was hungry most of the days. She asked for more bread, each time Neska screamed at her, "Don't you have enough?"

"But my father said I could eat much as I wanted, now you do not allow me to have more bread, I am hungry."

"Go to work, and you will have more tomorrow," Neska with her ugly, mean face said.

Several weeks passed by when after breakfast Hanka took Stas outside to the barn. Maria sneaked over the attic, and slowly walked over to the kitchen side and found a small hole in the ceiling. She lay down over the boards and peeped through a small opening and watched Neska as she took the loaf of bread and walked toward the cabinet and grabbed a knife from the counter and carved a cross on top of the loaf bread and took butter. Then she replaced them into the cabinet. She locked the cabinet and hid the key above the cabinet. That moment some dust from the celling fell down, and Maria was very scared; she did not move as Neska looked up. Neska once more looked up at the celling and walked towards the door, Maria carefully and quickly moved to the side behind the storage box of grain and waited. As Neska got closer to the attic steps the cat jumped from the last step and bounced against Neska's leg. With anger Neska almost kick him down but the cat escaped outside. Maria waited a little longer until she was sure that Neska was not at home, then she ran downstairs to the kitchen and quickly looked at the window and saw Neska entering the barn. Maria took the chair and climbed to get the key. She opened the cabinet, grabbed the bread and cut across a thick piece then again carved the cross over. From that day she hid some more bread for Stas and Hanka.

It was the end of October when Maria gathered her basic supplies, salt, and one small bag potatoes to bring to Jakob. She quickly placed the items in her school bag, hiding from stepmother. Lunch was almost ready, and she did not want to make her stepmother angry. At the first chance, Maria took off for the cave. Closer to the cave, she whispered, "Mr. Jackob, Mr. Jackob," and stepped over the rocks. The rocks moved under her foot slid down and made a cracking noise. She slowly moved behind the bushes and again softly called, "Mr. Jackob, are you here?"

When Jackob heard Maria, he quickly stepped out of the cave and welcomed her.

"You are Mr. Jackob?"

"Yes, I am Jackob, Maria."

"You look much different," Maria said. "I could not recognize you with full hair and your face covered by a beard."

"Why are you alone, Maria?" Jackob asked.

"Yes, I am alone. The SS took my father; the SS accused him for helping the partisans. All that is left at home is my stepmother with Hanka and Stas. One woman who knows my stepmother delivered sad news that my father was taken by the Nazi Army to the Eastern Front. I am so scared. I do not know if he ever comes back. My stepmother is very mean to me. She hides from me food and forces me to work hard in the stable, and every day I have to cut the firewood and clean the barn. I wish I could stay with you, but I must go back to my home. I do not have any other place to go."

There was nothing Jackob could do other than offer comfort to Maria. How could a man on the run offer any solace to a little girl?

A few days later, the Nazi police showed up at Michal's farm. They ordered Maria and her family out of the house. "You have ten minutes to gather your personal belongings and leave the premises. From now on, your farm is the property of the German Nation. We have a list of all your property. How many cows do you have? We know you have horse and farm equipment."

Ten minutes passed quickly. "Maria, are you ready?" Neska yelled across the room.

"Yes, Mom," Maria softly said, "I will be there in a minute," and she looked for her favorite long skirt. She found her skirt in the bottom of the dresser and quickly dropped it into her bundle and said, "Why has this this happened, my father is gone and now I do not know where I will be, Tato, my Tato," she cried as she looked at the photo. She grabbed it and wrapped it with her shirt and hid it in her white bundle. Neska nervously looked at the Nazi with his wristwatch, "Maria, are you coming?" Neska again called on her.

Maria lifted the bundle, slung it over her shoulder, and walked to the room. Rous, the Nazi commanded the family to quickly leave the house, as the kitchen door was wide open. Neska was pushed to walk to the front of the walkway towards the road and Maria was the last as Hanka with Stas were in front of her. Near the edge of the road, the Nazi commander directed them to join the other evicted families from the upper village and walked towards the center of the village plaza as the SS motorcycle escorted them. They reached the plaza and Maria noticed that there were no young men in the crowd, just women, children and the elderly. The SS never wasted time and wrapped all villagers into one large group then selected the younger and stronger to travel for work. Maria, and other children her age, were included in the first group. Neska, Anna and Stas were selected to stay in the village and the SS moved them to live with another family at the end of the village in a very small house.

Maria and the other children with the stronger elders were transported to the railroad station. Maria could see the trains and the thick smoke belched by the engines. Some of the trains Maria recognized as cattle cars. She also saw several other trucks with children and old people. Maria and the children were ordered out of the truck. They were marched behind others who were carrying suitcases and other small bundles. Maria held tightly onto her own bundle.

Soldiers were guarding the building. They were everywhere with vicious shepherds dogs tied on leashes, as they frequently barked ready to strike the nearest passengers as they stared at the crowd. Maria carefully stepped up over the cobblestones when the shepherd pulled hard at his leash from the guard towards Maria. Maria quickly looked the dog in the eye and said, "Get out, get out," showing no fear.

The guard, surprised by Maria's reaction, moved his head. "Brave girl," he said and pulled his dog back.

It was already crowded in the railroad station when the doors burst open as more people were forced inside. It was so jammed with people that there was hardly any room to stand. Bodies jostled against bodies. The crowd surged forward, pushing Maria between an old man and an old woman. The old man stumbled and the old woman was pushed by and SS. The old man tried to pull his luggage and fought hard to keep it with him. The lock broke and the luggage fell open dumping all the contents onto the floor. He hollered and screamed, "Let me have my briefcase!" but was too late. He looked behind as he saw all his belongings all over the floor and his small framed family photos broken in pieces. No one could help him to recover as the guards were shoving the crowds forward, all the time shouting, "Move, move! Move, Move!" Maria was swept along with the crowd.

She managed to free herself from the crowd and found herself on the train station platform. From the corner of her eye, Maria could see the man begging the guards to let him find his luggage. The guards showed him his broken luggage, and then ordered him into the cattle car.

Another guard directed Maria and others to a waiting SS guard. He blew his whistle and waved to them. He pointed to the cattle cars then yelled, "Go over there!" Maria was scared. The cattle car stunk of manure and packed tightly with other passengers. Over the next couple of hours, the cattle cars were continually loaded with people. Finally, when the cattle cars could hold no more, the doors were closed and locked.

The train locomotive operator waited for the commander at the station who stood near the first wagon and held in his hand a small red flag, then saw signs from the capo at the end of the last wagon ready to go. He dropped his left flag down. The operator of the locomotive pulled down the whistle cord and the train slowly left the station with thin black rising smoke. The passengers were startled. "The train is going to the north!" one of the men yelled. "We all are going to Auschwitz, we are not going to work on the farms and German camps."

The crowded wagon exploded with screams and great fear when an elder man loudly said, "We are not going to work on the farm, the train is going north to Auschwitz," and he placed his fingers between the boards and pulled trying to break them. He was too weak as the others helped him. The boards were very strong to break them down with bare hands. Some passengers stepped on each other letting the man get help. They kneeled down to the floor boards and looked on how to take the floor slabs apart when the train suddenly stopped and threw the man against the crowd. One woman who stood close to Maria screamed, "why do we stop now?" Then she heard another whistle while the workers changed the railroad tracks and positioned them back. The train moved a little farther and then started to move towards the south.

For a moment inside the wagon the passengers calmed down. "We are not going to Auschwitz."

Maria look at the elderly woman.

"No, my dear, we are not going to Auschwitz, we will be safe," she said to Maria as she looked at the rest of the tired and weary men and women and teenage girls and boys.

As fall ended, Jakob began to be worried about the safety of his hiding place. The leaves were turning, and he knew that soon enough that the vegetation that sheltered his cave would die off. He looked at the site and carefully walked over the stream and crossed towards the other side to collect pine needles to drop them near his cave. Then he picked some of the low lying bushes and carefully swept behind his footsteps until he reached the cave.

Jakob wasn't worried about his survival over the winter. He had prepared well. He knew that the short days and long nights would be his worst hurdle to overcome. Snow began to fall, blocking what little sunlight remained. Jakob made a small fire in the stone stove, knowing that no Nazi patrol would be searching in such a storm. He lay down on his makeshift bed, his thoughts drifting to his life and better times before the war. Wolves were baying in the hills. The sound of their cries shook Jakob to his core and echoed his loneliness.

During the long winter, many times Jakob touched his face and felt his growing beard. He wondered how he looked, and imagined he looked like a hermit. He paced from wall to wall seeking for comfort when his mind raced against the time. He tried to sleep longer and tried to avoid his sadness of losing all his family and friends from the camp. Then he thought, *what is better to live like a hermit and have no one to talk to and share his feelings or to be on death row?* But each time with his horrified thoughts he remembered the old prisoner's hands in the camp, and thought, *I will survive, I must tell.* The flash of his wife with children and last embrace with them held his spirit on. I have to be strong, and he prayed placing his head against the wall. It seemed to Jakob that winter went on forever until he saw the first signs of spring. He could hear water rushing in the creek near his cave.

The Nazis brought Maria and other workers to a site of unfinished long trenches. Maria briefly watched the cold wind blowing the snow against the forest line from the hillside and the group of men carried with them over their shoulders logs of wood and followed the Nazi guards who staked the line for trenches. The other group pulled behind heavy wheels wrapped with barbed wire. They nailed the barbwire against the wooden posts and the others built the trench hundreds of feet away from the forest line. Teenager boys with Maria and other girls with hundreds of older men received shovels and picks, and then were forced to work in a partially finished trench near the forest. Maria overheard workers who she did not understand as they talked loud, until she moved inside the deep cut trench to avoid the frozen wind constantly blowing against her face. Her lips were trembling from the cold while she shoveled the snow from the bottom of the trench.

An old man who was working in the trenches saw Maria trembling, wanted to give her help and asked Maria in Polish, "What is your name and where do you come from?"

"I am from Bystra," Maria said.

"Oh, I know your village. I am from Zywiec, and I have been there. Nazis surrounded my neighbors and gave us little time to prepare our basic needs and then we were escorted to the train station, then brought to this place by dirty wagon trains with others from my town. My wife is working at the village not far away from here, but I do not see any of my neighbors."

"What is your name Mr.?" Maria asked.

"Marian," and he continued telling his story. "I was in this same group of people as you." As he worked, he continued to talk with Maria, always looking over his shoulder to make sure that the guards were not watching him. All of a sudden, Maria jumped up in an effort to keep her hands warm. "Be careful," Marian said."

He talked to Maria while he removed the rubble of cut stones from frozen ground. Each time dumping the rubble over the edge of the trench, then he looked towards the guards on both side of the ditches as they walked along the trench. Then he quit talking when the guard saw Maria again jump up and down to keep her warm as the guard walked toward them. "Be careful," the older men said to Maria, "the guard is coming."

This time Maria quickly grabbed the shovel and pushed the snow away from the top edges of the trench, and when she rose up with the stone she saw the guard's long boots at the edge of trench. She stepped a few feet away from the edge, afraid that he may slip over to her side. Maria briefly looked at him as his dog shook powdery snow over him held by the guard. The guard bent above the trench towards Maria's side. "Come over here," he called on her, "come here, give me your hand." He took his gloves off as Maria grabbed his warm hand, as she was pulled from the trench she turned her head towards the workers shivering and afraid, and looked at the elderly man and several others near the side as they proceeded with their work. He pulled her from the trench and dropped over her shoulder an old coat he carried with him. "Come; come," several times he said, as Maria could understand as he shoved his hand toward her. Maria wrapped herself with the coat and held her hands inside the pockets near her stomach, then walked with the guard towards the forest line. Maria felt a little warmer but the wind brushed against her face as her lips trembled and she could not stop. As the trench line ended behind the hills Maria walked faster to keep warm, until they were closer to the forest, and the guard stopped her by pulling her arm from behind and switched his gun from his right arm to his left. He removed from his pocket a small wallet. "Maria," he said, "come closer to me." She took a look at his sad face as he opened the wallet wide, then he said, "Look at these two photos with two pretty young girls, Hitler caput, Hitler Caput," he said. "These are my girls," he kissed them and put them to his heart, "these are my children," and he almost wept. "They are at your age," he repeated, "and I miss them a lot. I do not want to be here, the Nazis forced me, and others to be here. We all must suffer and why I am here? I have my own home. Look at the forest," he said, "behind there is a small farm, go over there and get warm." Then he looked into the sky, and said, "When it gets darker, you must come back to report here."

She ran fast towards the woods, then turned into the short curved path into the barn. The barn attached into the stable in the back of the house, she slowly opened the door and the warm air she felt quickly, and she slipped inside the barn as the cows mooed. Shortly after she entered, the ice melted from her frozen boots and her face warmed up and turned red as she wrapped her wet hair down. She was very hungry, and squeezed herself between two cows staying in the row and rubbed her hands against them. She kneeled below one cow and milked her, as the milk flowed into her mouth, oh, she took for moment her breath; it was warm and she pulled a few more times, and touched the belly of the cows as they moved their tails strong towards Maria and stood quietly as she knew that Maria was hungry and cold. Shortly after, Maria heard someone coming in. She rushed away from the cows and hid behind two wooden coffers near the wall, and covered herself with hay. When the farmer opened the door, she felt the cold breeze. Fortunately, he quickly closed the door, walked towards the coffers, filed with the large jars of corn, and gave it to the cows. Maria sat very quietly as the cows turned their heads toward her as she saw them well from behind as the farmer cleaned around the manure and placed around some straw. He looked around the stable as if he felt Maria's presence; after a while he left.

Maria lay down on the hay until late afternoon, and looked through the stable window and tracked the daylight. Then she realized that she had to return to the trenches and report at the end of work. She rushed through the woods and sneaked inside the end of trenches while some workers already were ready to form a group for the departure. The soldier guard saw her briefly and only winked his eye to her letting her know that everything is all right. The older man was happy to see Maria, that she returned safe and that she was alive, he liked her even though he knew her very little.

Maria reported to work and each time the guard was looking for her and secretly always asked her to go to the end of the trench near the forest.

It was end of the March 1945 when the workers on the trench detail saw a squadron of planes fly overhead. They were dropping bombs. Everyone ran for cover. The workers ran towards the village then turned at the small lines of trees. Then the other squadrons of planes circled around and dropped more bombs over the trenches.

Maria ran towards the forest about a half mile away. The others followed. The next wave of airplanes dropped more bombs. Maria fell to the ground and covered her head with her hands. She waited for the bombs to stop. The others start to run again, but Maria stayed still. The old man quickly pulled her up. "Come quickly," he said to Maria. They made it to the forest and finally felt safe from the bombs. She looked behind and saw ball of fire and smoke from the side of the trenches and the farm. The raid of the planes lasted until late afternoon, with the cold all workers hid behind the forest line and stayed inside the bushes to keep warm. As the raid stopped, one elder man led the workers towards the village. "We must get some food and warmer clothes," he said as they walked across the craters left after the bombing and found few empty houses. They found some food and collected in baskets from the barns they what they found. "We must reach the rail station and return home."

Maria quickly followed the elder man wrapped with burlap and a basket of food. "How far to the station?" Maria asked the elder man.

"Two miles, my child, we will be there soon."

They walked across the frozen fields, then saw the smoke from the rail station building; it was not bombed. The group of workers reached the station and quickly entered the big waiting room with some children shaking from the cold. At the station there were more people waiting for the train to arrive. Then an hour later, Maria with her other friend, hollered over, "The train is coming, we can go home now."

As the train arrived there were many people returning from the south. Maria with her group entered to the passenger wagons as all were greeted by strangers. "The war is over. Hitler lost!" the other people said loudly.

The train moved towards the Polish border, then stopped, the bridge was destroyed, and all the passengers left to take the rest of the journey by foot. Maria's group stuck together as the leader and the elderly man directed them towards the forest line. The passage through the dark forest made everyone in the group very tired. Maria with her little strength extended her hands to help an elderly woman to climb over some of the rocks. "I hope we will get to the village soon," the woman said to her and looked behind her as the rest of them slowly climbed over the stretched narrow path.

"Can we get rest?" some of the elders called from the end of the line.

As they walked a little farther, the guide reached the top of the hill at the edge of the forest, and yelled, "I see the village, we made it, I see the village!" as everyone from the group rose above their weakness.

"We made it!" one man called to others and embraced him.

Maria with the other girls rushed towards the end of the forest edge and stopped when they saw in the distance several airplanes flying over the village. They all waited until the guide said, "We are safe, and we can go down to the village."

"Mr. Tadek, how far are we from Bystra do you know?" Maria with the other girls asked.

"It is still far, we are just crossed inside Poland and your village is far away, another two days or so to walk. But do not worry you will get there," he said as he saw Maria and the girls' sad faces.

"I want to go to my home, to see my sister with brother, I do not know where they are, I so hope to find them alive."

"Don't worry, Maria," he said.

"I must find Jackob, he hides inside the mountain. He must be alive, he must."

"Who is Jackob?" the man asked.

"He is the man who came to my home, and asked for help, he was wounded, he was shot by the Nazis and my father took him to hiding in the forest. I trust him, he knew my father and my father may be dead, he never returned home. I must find Jackob."

The group entered the dirt road and slowly passed several burned sheds and houses with skeletons of roofs. They entered the village without signs of life until they saw one building with rising chimney smoke.

"We must be careful to walk farther," the old man said. "I must go first and find out who is in that home." The others were listening him, and sat near over the grass field and waited for the guide.

"What happened to the people?" one elderly woman asked as they were talking and planning to return to their homes.

The man reached the home and was welcomed by an old couple. "What are you doing here?"

"I am here with a hungry group of people who walked across the mountains escaping the front."

"The Russians were here, they moved their tanks and arms. Many of them fought hard. They came without shoes, only wrapped with heavy cloth and they were angry and vicious to kill all Germans settled in the village, the German settlers ran away fast leaving their belongings afraid to lose their lives and some of the buildings they put on fire before they left. As you can see the home across the road. We do not have much food, but we can share whatever we have," the elderly woman said.

With the spring warmer weather and sound of the creek, it made Jackob go out earlier. Each day he got up with hope that Maria will visit him. He was able to walk out of the cave more often. His food supplies could last for another month. He rationed carefully each portion of grain for breakfast and potatoes for the rest of the day. He planned to sneak inside the village and collect more food.

Every day carefully he walked between the thick woods and bushes down the hill towards the village and sat near the edge of the forest line and from a distance, he could see the village. Over two weeks he carefully observed the site with temptation to sneak in to collect food. These days Jackob enjoyed most as he saw the opportunity to be outside and enjoy nature and his hope to rejoin his family and his little friend Maria.

In late April, several airplanes interrupted Jackob's trip to the edge of the forest as they flew over the village valley, and followed by church bells, loud enough echoing across the valley. For while he could not understand why these bells were ringing and stood over the edge of the forest; then from a distance towards the road he saw groups of villagers. This must be a celebration of some kind. The Nazis never permitted the villagers to form groups he recalled from the Nazi orders after they occupied the region. Still, he hesitated to go and explore these events. He decided to return to his cave.

The next day, he went to other side edge of the forest at the nearest entry to the village just at the forest line. When he saw two men with their rifles walk freely around old house, he left the side of the woods and called, "Hello, my fellows."

They turned against him with their rifles pointed at him. "Who are you?" they called.

They were shocked to see bearded Jackob. "I am Jackob, I am hiding in the forest, what is going on in the village?" Jackob asked. "I saw from the hills that they are free to move around; I heard the bells and airplanes flying over the valley. Can you please tell me what happened?"

The men looked at each other. "Don't you know, the Nazis are gone from the region, the Russians pushed them back, we are free."

Jackob fell at their knees and then embraced both of them. "I am free, I am finally free!" he cried, and he took a deep breath.

"This village is Bystra?" he asked the men.

"No, Bystra is on the other side the hills."

"I must see Michal's farm."

"Michal's farm is no longer there; we knew him. The Nazis took him and others of our friends."

"But Maria his daughter must be there," Jackob insisted. "She must be there."

One of the men replied, "The Nazis wrapped up most of the families last year and took them to Germany to work."

Then the other man paused and said, "But we heard that many are returning from the west. You may find Maria and her family if they survived."

"I must find Maria. I must."

The men showed him shortcuts to Maria's village across the hills. "You are now safe.

Jackob with high emotions left the men until he reached the top of the hills and saw Maria's village. For a moment, he paused and then closed his eyes. He shivered, and was scared, *what if I cannot find Maria*, he thought. From the hills, Jackob reached the narrowed dirt road to the center of village. He passed several burned houses until he saw a group of people gathered inside a small farmhouse. From the side of the adjacent road, another group of people with small wagons crossed over the road and arrived at the house, they were returning to their homes. They stopped at the house to get some fresh water and get some rest. The group came from the east side. Jackob asked several women, "Do you live in this village?"

"No, we are stopping over here and we must go to our home towards the west."

Jackob again asked, "Do you know if anyone returned from the Germans? I am looking for Maria. I must find her."

They all looked at the bearded Jackob. "We do not know who Maria is."

"The little girl," Jackob said, "she is Michal's daughter."

No one knew them. Then a woman from the house stepped out from the house and overheard. "Michal's farm? He is no longer there; his wife is there," she said.

Jackob drank some water and rushed through the village, as he was close over the hilly side of the road he recognized the farm and burned barns and damaged Michal's roof house. He stopped near the oak tree above the field as his mind flashed to the moment when Michal gave him first aid. *I hope Maria will be there.* He slowly entered inside the court and heard Stas scream, "Mom, Mom, someone is here!"

Neska saw Jackob, but she could not recognize him. "What are you looking for?" she asked Jackob.

"I am Jackob."

"What, you are Jackob, you are alive." Not so happy, Neska said, "You must go away from here."

"Where is Maria?" Jacob asked.

"She is dead, she is no longer here."

"No, she must be alive."

"The Nazis took her to a labor camp. She must be dead, she never returned."

"I will look for Maria," he said. "She must return here. This is her farm." "What? This is *my* farm, and no one will take the farm from me."

"What about Stas? And Hanka?"

Jackob felt unwelcome in Michal's farm. "I will find Maria, she will come back to the farm," he reiterated to Neska. "She loved this farm, she must return. But what for, don't you see there is nothing left the barn is burned and the horses are gone, Neska replied" Jackob with sadness and anger waked away and with disbelief shook his head. As he reached the center of the village he met two men. "Do you know if some villagers from the upper side of village returned to their homes? I am looking for Maria."

"There is a group of people returning from the Czech and German labor camps. They are coming with children and Maria may be with them."

Jackob thanked the men and with his hope to meet Maria, he decided to wait in the village.

Jackob left Neska with great disappointment that Maria was not at her house and walked towards the village center. At the center, he found a group of men and women standing and discussing their future. Jackob stopped. "Excuse me," he said to the group. "Do you have any news from Auschwitz?"

One man quickly said to Jackob, "Oh, Auschwitz; the Russians bombed Auschwitz, and they liberated them, that's what we only heard."

Then the other man said, "Many inmates were able to last minute escape."

"I must go there and find my wife and children, my boy and girl."

He walked for several days, then caught soldiers as they drove towards Auschwitz town. As he reached the town center, he saw many inmates still in their inmate's uniforms. As he walked between the inmates and searched for his wife and children one sanitary worker walked with the inmates and saw Jackob. "What are you doing here?"

"My wife my children, they were in the camp. I must look for them."

"No one is left in the camp. All of them left."

"But I must find my family. I will not have life without them," Jackob said. "You go over there, the barracks are destroyed, nothing is left over there." Jackob insisted, "But I must go. I know they survived."

When he reached the camp, and saw the skeletons of the barracks and the barbed wire fence apart, the smell of burning flesh overwelmed him, as he fell down rememberd his other priseners perished in the oven only to be seen in the dark black smoke from the tall chimney still standing toll. The railroad tracks he remembered never ended as he flashed in his memories of his family were the Naziz teared them apart. He stood and opened his arms wide. He loudly cried, "My wife, do you hear me?" He pauses for a moment took his deep breath, shocked his shiver body, and said, I must find my family and Maria, the girl who saved my life.

WALTER JURASZEK

Walter is native of Poland. At age 14, he left his family farm, joining a surveying and engineering firm to become an engineering surveyor for the Polish Infrastructure Ministry. His job enabled him to travel across the country, where he worked with and explored the lives of ordinary people from factory workers to farmers as well as high level communist party officials and university educators. As he witnessed the socialist/communist system shape humans into classes, not individuals, he noted the behavior of the political system which served well the communist establishment. A keen observer with great interest in world affairs and captivated by Radio Free Europe and the Voice of America. For several years, he planned his escape from Poland.

Walter, a legal immigrant, become a naturalized American citizen in 1985, and is practicing civil engineer. He risked his life to escape from communism, a compelling story, in its own right, of one man's struggle.

He arrived in New York City penniless, without family or friends, and without speaking English. He found shelter in the Manhattan subway with homeless people and quickly learn basic English. Since then he worked as rooms hotels painter, janitor, in Manhattan, technician in Petroleum company in Oklahoma, Civil Engineering firm in Raleigh North Carolina, Department of Transportation. Working during the day, he continued study engineering at night. He also was assigned to a team by the USDOT to work in Moscow with Russian Ministry of Transportation and the World Bank officials to help Russian Government in transition from centralized economy to free market in transportation construction industries after the Communism Soviet Union collapsed. He has become fluent in English, Spanish, Russian as well as Polish. He holds Civil Engineering Degree and Master of Science in civil Engineering. He travels across the U.S. and the World and explores all walks of people's lives.